DATING YOURSELF

DATING YOURSELF

FINDING SELF-LOVE
BEFORE TRUE LOVE

MATTHEW HENRY

NEW DEGREE PRESS

DATING YOURSELF
Finding Self-Love Before True Love

ISBN   978-1-64137-960-1   *Paperback*
        978-1-64137-783-6   *Kindle Ebook*
        978-1-64137-784-3   *Ebook*

CONTENTS

———

INTRODUCTION: SELF-LOVE BEFORE TRUE LOVE

———

Dating has transformed dramatically over the years due to the birth and accelerated use of social media and smartphone dating applications. These new technologies have altered the way we communicate, making the ability to socialize and even date people a much more instantaneous experience. Technology can absolutely make life easier and even produce success stories of people finding the love of their lives via online channels. However, we also have to recognize there is a dark side to online communication and interaction, to a point where our happiness can be negatively impacted.

An unfortunate byproduct of some dating apps is they can reduce mature, loyal, hardworking people into contestants in a competition of hotness. There is much more to a person than meets the eye, let alone making an instant decision of whether or not to swipe right.

This is not a book purely on dating apps or dating itself. Rather, this book's purpose is to help you explore how to find true love by falling in love with the most important person in the world: **you**! That's right—**your self-happiness is what will drive the happiness and long-term health of your future relationships**.

A July 2019 survey conducted by Match.com indicated that out of the 5,001 US adult participants, 63 percent of millennials (born between 1981 and 1996) and 70 percent of Gen Z (born after 1996) daters are looking for a serious relationship. The flip side is millennials and Gen Z'ers are also satisfied with staying single.[1]

Dr. Darcy Sterling, Tinder's relationship expert, claims *"millennials invest more time in careers, social lives and personal time when single. They appreciate that periods without a partner give them more time to cultivate other arenas of their lives."*[2] Other reasons for accepting the single life include being unbridled from commitments that may impair the opportunity to have new experiences and placing a high value on feeling empowered through independence.

As a young adult, I've been told frequently by my elders the biggest investment I would make in life is purchasing a home. As I've navigated through the world of dating and after conversing with many married, divorced, and unmarried young couples, I now subscribe to the idea that **the biggest**

---

1   Joshua Bote, "Millennial and Gen Z singles have enough casual sex. But they want love, survey says," *USA Today*, July 29, 2019.

2   Nora Battelle, "Young People Are Staying Single for These 3 Reasons, According to New Research," *Thrive Global*, October 10, 2018.

investment a person will make in their lifetime is the partner they choose to spend the rest of their life with.

That one person we deem to be special will become an intricate part of our lives. As the relationship continues, that special someone will take the time to know your parents, siblings, extended family members, best friends, and most importantly, they will take time to understand your deepest feelings and insecurities. It is not easy to be this vulnerable with anyone, which is why finding a person you authentically **trust** and **love** is the most important investment you will ever make in your lifetime.

While spending time with this person, you will also begin to slowly adopt each other's habits, behaviors, social circles, lifestyle, and time. I understand finding all of this information about any individual does not happen overnight, but when entering the world of dating it is important to understand yourself first so you can better understand the person you are bringing into your life.

Personally, writing a book about dating and self-happiness was far from my mind about a year ago. On November 24, 2018, I published my first book titled *Working Together: Why We Need Bipartisanship in American Politics*. What I discovered in covering politics, as well as interviewing high-profile government officials over that year-long duration, was we have a major problem with empathetic messaging and communication. It did not matter which political party someone belonged to, but the fact we were so divided socially is what has contributed to the polarization in our state and national politics.

Months after my first book was published, I flirted with the concept of perhaps writing a second book, but this time it would be on a completely different subject. I was always fascinated and curious with the current dating landscape, so what better way to learn more about it than to write a book about it! When I officially made the decision to pursue writing another book, I was hesitant at first about the subject matter and backed away from the topic altogether. I did not want to be placed in the same category as some other authors who wrote on this topic, simply because I was not a fan of nor did I want to be associated with the labels "guru" or "dating expert." I disregarded writing about the topic for a while until I started making a connection between the world of politics and the world of dating. Similar to how American political parties are polarized ideologically, I started to see trends dividing men and women.

When I would hang out with couples who were close friends, I often felt they miscommunicated some of their most intimate feelings towards each another. What was even more surprising was they felt comfortable enough confiding in me about their problems, while simultaneously feeling too distant to share those problems with their partner. Despite these small realizations, I still wasn't committed to writing a book about dating just yet, until one day at a party, my closest friends once again began opening up about their relationship problems. They shared a lot of similarities in terms of their frustration with communication; even those in long-term, serious relationships expressed similar concerns. One day, while drinking an old-fashioned, I had that "aha" moment. I had the sudden realization this lack of communication in dating is a much bigger problem than expected, and definitely needed to be talked about in the form of a book.

One of my best friends, Emma Earnest, a former actress and model who used to live in Los Angeles, shared her relationship stories with me. She told me about needing to initiate the breakup but not following through because *"it was simply too difficult at the time."* The result was she stayed in that relationship longer than she should have, which led to arguments that didn't need to happen. Emma expressed, *"the hardest part is hurting that person's feelings, even though you know it's for the best."*

It didn't stop there with just my closest girlfriends; even my "bros" had a difficult time when it came to communicating in a relationship. The problems they were facing involved transition periods or having different goals for the future. I found myself beginning to ruminate on the idea there was a much deeper meaning in relationships than just being physically attracted to someone or sharing common interests. The need to cultivate a deep connection, understand each other's personal goals, show actions of empathy, and provide higher levels of emotional support were the common denominators between both my girl and guy friends as the primary reasons why they felt unsatisfied in their relationships.

My friends were some of the most important catalysts who inspired me to write this book. It has truly been a transformative experience not only hearing their experiences in dating, but also listening to their stories of personal struggles and how their characters were shaped through the obstacles life threw at them. In this book, we will take some time to read about their stories, the lessons they learned, as well as look at how we can identify troublesome patterns so we can learn from their mistakes.

Everyone deserves to be happy and feel loved, yet those are two emotions that at times can feel distant and unattainable. So, how do we make ourselves feel these emotions? What is the recipe for success and happiness? For one, it takes a lot of work in the self-improvement department in terms of being self-disciplined and taking the time to work on yourself emotionally, intellectually, and even physically.

Self-love does not come without action and does not happen by simply "faking it." Self-love is a journey that involves finding out more about yourself. As we've gotten older, we've developed unconscious habits that slowly shape the way we behave. The truth is we can either keep or change those habits. It's all up to us. By practicing healthier habits that are not toxic to our mental health, we can then begin to experience the benefits of loving ourselves. These benefits are long-lasting, and not only will it make you happier, but it might also make your relationships more romantic.

A good metaphor I like to think of in terms of taking care of your own happiness was actually shared with me by a friend's mother: At the beginning of any commercial flight, the flight attendants will explain that, in an emergency, the only way to help the child next you is by first putting on your oxygen mask. For me, this exemplifies the idea that **you must take care of your own well-being first in order to help others**.

This book will look at the benefits of self-happiness before entering a relationship through advice from married and divorced couples, psychologists within the fields of interpersonal communication, and people currently immersed in the dating scene. I will also briefly discuss my former battle with depression, and how being grateful and helping those less fortunate was a catalyst for saving my life while also helping me on my own journey of self-love.

If you are in your twenties to early thirties and are still oscillating between being in a relationship and living the single life, I believe this book will be of great benefit to you in terms of guiding you on how to be happier with what you have and to further develop ways to achieve your maximum happiness potential.

Young people in this day and age can be faced with a unique set of social challenges, particularly when it comes to the dating scene. For example, Ashton Nadine, a young professional from Fairfax, Virginia, says that being a different skin color has played a role in her dating life. She explains "*for some men, I could be a first or an experiment, someone they couldn't even bring home to their parents. They mention things like 'I have never been with a Black woman before' which is the ultimate turn off. I've lately been putting more effort into meeting Black and mixed men to relate on a cultural and social level.*"

Physical or cultural differences should never play a role in being judged beforehand. A barrier into why we may not find the person of our dreams is we might find ourselves unconsciously biased against those of a different nationality and/ or race. I hope you, the reader, will be honest with yourself while at the same time not being judgmental of others. People are not social experiments and shouldn't be treated as such. Commitments in relationships need to be taken seriously if you truly want to establish a healthy relationship.

No matter what race, religion, education, sexual orientation, or moral beliefs you may have, the lessons I've learned from others can possibly transform your life if you allow it. Think of this as a take-action journal. The lessons from this book are from real couples and experts who have been transparent about their experiences and research. **Dating another person is a major lifestyle change and investment in your life. It is important to understand yourself first before signing up to take care of someone else**.

On the topic of self-love, Ashton has practiced a healthy approach when it comes to taking care of herself as she explains: *"I've learned that dating should result in me adding more fun experiences to my life. If my 'self' isn't aligned, I'll take a break from dating."*

The purpose of this book is to detail the importance of self-love and fulfillment before entering a long-term relationship. Finding a partner can be difficult, but it doesn't have to be a stressful journey. The journey of self-love and finding your true love is a beautiful adventure. So sit back, relax, and let's make you better!

PART I

HOW WE GOT HERE

CHAPTER 1

THE DAYS BEFORE SOCIAL MEDIA AND DIGITAL DATING

———

Searching for the love of your life has now become a much more instantaneous process since the days our parents got hitched. Back in those days, the typical protocol for initiating contact involved asking a potential partner for their phone number, which sometimes would mean calling the family house phone (no smartphones back then). From our perspective, meeting a new person in those days would seem like a daunting challenge that would require more effort than we may be used to. In our current dating scene, simply following someone on Twitter, liking an Instagram picture, or sending a message on Facebook is enough to set up a friendly in-person meeting at a coffee shop. We now have a plethora of options for gaining access to potential partners with just a couple of taps on our smartphones.

Despite the evolution of dating through smartphone technology, why does it still seem so hard to date?

Why are some of us still single? Do we suck? Or are we of such high caliber we need to interrogate others who are worthy of our loyalty and love?

One of the main reasons dating is harder for millennials and Gen Z'ers is we face insurmountable pressure to take care of our professional careers, which typically require years of experience while also dealing with other responsibilities, such as paying off student loans and, much like other generations, adapting to an evolving technological environment. We will speak more about this in later chapters.

First, when it comes to the dating process, we need to exercise **patience**. Similar to any other major financial investment we make in our lives, dating requires us to perform reconnaissance on ourselves and the people we are trying to pursue so we know what fit feels right. The numbers work in everyone's favor (ideally), because all it takes is one person to fall in love with (unless you are polyamorous).

The lack of access to new people (depending on our location) can sometimes feel as if we are at a major disadvantage in comparison to relationship seekers living in more populated rural or city environments. A potential downfall of this ability to find dates instantly is when people don't look like people anymore and they begin to look like options on a Netflix menu. Because we are exposed to a wealth of social and technological resources, potential mates can become saturated in an already overpopulated market.

Learning about people can take months and is a gradual, not an instant, process. More importantly, we need to understand and accept dating is a process which involves **uncovering potentially harmful Red Flags sooner rather than later.**

The idea of utilizing matchmaking services to find the person of our dreams has been around long before the invention of the smartphone and even the World Wide Web. Since the 1940s, companies have been using data as a blueprint for matchmaking services. World War II had a major impact on dating during that time, as later there would be a shortage of men. The *New York Times* in June 1945 *"predicted 750,000 women who wanted to marry would have to live alone."*[3] Because of this scarcity in male partners, marriage rates began to augment. Post-war dating also witnessed another significant change where both men and women were beginning to get married at a much younger age; approximately eighteen for women and twenty years old for men.

A website called Kiss.com would become the first ever dating website, which would soon be followed by the more popular Match.com in 1995; the birth of these two sites would then spark a sudden burst of sixteen new dating websites the following year. In 2004, four Harvard students would develop OkCupid, which is a website and iPhone application that is still around today. OkCupid would sort of serve as a catalyst for other well-known dating apps; Tinder ushered in a whole a new era for digital dating since its 2013 release on all smartphones.

---

3   Skip Burzumato, "A Brief History of Courtship and Dating in America, Part 2," *Boundless*, March 8, 2007.

Ashley Fetters from *The Atlantic* writes:

"In 2018, seven of the 53 couples profiled in the Vows column met on dating apps. And in the Times' more populous Wedding Announcements section, 93 out of some 1,000 couples profiled this year met on dating apps—Tinder, Bumble, Hinge, Coffee Meets Bagel, Happn, and other specialized dating apps designed for smaller communities, like JSwipe for Jewish singles and MuzMatch for Muslims. The year before, 71 couples whose weddings were announced by the Times met on dating apps."[4]

The danger of digital profiles is they make it harder to uncover the flaws of a person (feel free to disagree). If you're a woman, then the digital age has dramatically changed how men can communicate with you. Men, because of online data, are able to access your social profiles or even your email if they simply know your name. Most of the time there is no danger present; however, it does make it much easier for strangers to contact you. As a result of technology, hackers can also gain access to your personal information, particularly social media accounts. Even though some platforms give users the option of setting a privacy mode, hackers are still able to maneuver around these digital barriers.

Dating, before social media, essentially required much more effort than it does today. How so? Well, as stated earlier, it was much harder to send a "Hey, what's up?" message to anyone, let alone a potential partner. Communication sometimes

---

4   Ashley Fetters, "The Five Years That Changed Dating," *The Atlantic*, December 21, 2018.

involved knowing a mutual friend who would help "set you up." Blind dates were, in a sense, truly blind dates, unlike today where so much of our information is already established online and you can perform a "dating reconnaissance" on someone you might be going on a date with. Old Facebook or Instagram photos can be used either for or against you because those old pictures can resurface at any time if someone chooses to search your name; on the flip side, you can also do the same with a person you wish to learn more about (#dontbeastalker).

Speaking of stalkers, the old era of dating did have one major advantage: no fake online profiles. There are, unfortunately, some dangerous elements to this new digital arena, such as the practice of "catfishing." A catfish profile is a fake profile with a real picture of someone else. Oftentimes individuals will pretend to be someone else to manipulate and attract people they want to date. Without the World Wide Web, it was much harder for creepers to bait and hook real people.

While not everyone is a victim of catfishing when they create a social media or dating account, character traits on profiles are much harder to detect early on due to the nature of instant swiping.

According to the Pew Research Center, "***millennials are starting families later than their counterparts in prior generations**. Just under half (46 perceent) of Millennials ages twenty-five to thirty-seven are married, a steep drop from the 83 percent of Silents* (born between 1928 and 1945) *who were married in 1968.*

The share of twenty-five- to thirty-seven-year-olds who were married steadily dropped for each succeeding generation, from 67 percent of early Boomers (born between 1946 and 1964) *to 57 percent of Gen Xers* (born between 1965 and 1980). *In 1968, the typical American woman first married at age twenty-one and the typical American man first wed at twenty-three. Today, those figures have climbed to twenty-eight for women and thirty for men.*"[5]

It is not by accident millennials are starting families later than previous generations. Financially, this and upcoming generations will have to face pressures to establish themselves professionally, in addition to having to pay for higher education. Because of the pressures to establish a steady career which may require years of experience before making a substantial income, along with paying off student loan debts, millennials have a major disadvantage before they even enter the dating scene.

The high cost of rent and mortgages are continuing to skyrocket, especially in affluent neighborhoods, making it much harder for younger couples to purchase homes. For example, when my parents first moved to the US in 1987, they rented an apartment in Tysons, Virginia, for approximately $600 a month. Now, that same one-bedroom apartment in 2020 has a lease rate of approximately $1,600 per month (utilities not included). This acceleration in housing costs is hurting millennials, who are also facing an alarming amount of student loan debt; "*in 2018, 15 percent of Millennials (ages*

5   Richard Fry and Kristen Bialik, "Millennial life: How young adulthood today compares with prior generations." Pew Research Center, accessed February 14, 2019.

twenty-five to thirty-seven) were living in their parents' home. This is nearly double the share of early Boomers and Silents (8 percent each) and 6 percentage points higher than Gen Xers who did so when they were the same age."[5]

Financial pressures to start a family will continue to become more difficult for millennials, but it does not mean the youth should entirely give up on the idea of starting a family. What makes this generation special is the ability to adapt and ignite change. We've witnessed this recently where students have quickly adjusted to online college and high school classes, changed their social habits by scheduling virtual happy hours, and helped ignite a cultural movement to take on systemic racism. Anything is possible with this current generation, which personally makes me feel optimistic about the future ahead. I've recently had a friend welcome his first daughter into the world during this global coronavirus pandemic. He made no excuses and did what he needed to do to protect his family. It was incredible to witness such strength from a man I used to party with. This exemplifies that we can accomplish and succeed in any scenario if we set our minds to it and focus.

The fear of dating and starting a family due to professional, financial, and social pressures is beginning to become a non-factor in terms of deterring millennials from starting a family. Even though these pressures still exist and will affect people in different ways, I believe that millennials will persevere and become amazing parents and leaders of the next generation.

CHAPTER 2

PROS AND CONS OF DATING APPS

———

Swipe right and you might meet your future wife or husband! That's what makes the concept of downloading and using dating apps so appealing. Almost operating as if it's a smartphone game that involves swiping through a deck of cards, this playful yet addictive game of romance roulette has revolutionized the dating scene.

Similar to social media usage, users can be swallowed into spending upwards of twenty hours per week swiping and messaging. While the possibility of meeting your next girlfriend or boyfriend could be one swipe or message away, the cost of constantly using these apps can become detrimental to one's productiveness and overall mental health. That same amount of time could be used more efficiently on activities that benefit self-improvement, exploring the world around you, or creating a new in-person connection (the same argument can also be applied to social media).

Alexis Kristok, a hairstylist, millennial mother, and good friend of mine, met her husband long before dating apps became popular in mainstream culture:

"My husband and I went on a date to Chipotle when we were sixteen years old. He brought a friend to our date for emotional support and, for that reason, we never really connected due to being third-wheeled. We, however, still remained distant friends and stayed connected socially. Years later, after many relationships on both ends and a mutual best friend, we reconnected...the rest is history"

While Alexis did not rely on using dating apps to meet her significant other, many of her friends have found success and are currently in a healthy place in their relationships. She explains:

"I have downloaded dating applications then deleted after one week personally, but my friends have had great success in finding their partner. One of my friends downloaded the Bumble app and matched with the man that is now her husband. They're madly in love and just had their baby girl during this pandemic"

There are benefits to using this technology, as long as it is being used in moderation and not taking time away from more important aspects of life (spending time with family and taking care of personal well-being). The digital capability to bring two people together who generally would not have access to each other is enough to make these apps worth at least a trial run.

Launched in 2012, Tinder is the most popular and commonly used dating app, which now has over ten million active users. Users navigate to find other men or women within their geographical range by using a criterion that can be customized to age and gender preference. Much like a Facebook profile, a user can upload photos and create a quick biography of who they are and what they are searching for in a desired partner. They can also view the photos and bios of other potential partners. If a match takes place, when both users swipe right on each other, only then will they be allowed to directly message each other. Tinder does have a reputation for being labeled a "hook up app," in which singles solely use the app for either one-night stands or short-term relationships; however, this does not mean Tinder has not helped people from forming lasting relationships.

For a group of women from Seattle, the creepy messages men sent on dating apps such as Tinder inspired them to create their own dating app called Siren. This app was designed to protect women against potential creepers who have a proclivity for sending vulgar and sexually explicit messages. Siren puts the woman in charge by getting rid of the swipe option and instead utilizing a "daily open-ended question" feature; if the female user likes the answer from the male participant, then she has the option of making her profile visible to him. Co-founder Susie Lee stated to *Business Insider* in an interview, *"the swiping interaction is fun, but when you apply that to people, you're reducing people to objects. Whether it's shoes or humans, you can do the same interaction: push them away or pull them closer. We want to fight this idea that you're shopping for humans."*[6]

The app generated over *"38,000 registered users, with an 80 percent response rate to initial messages."*[7] The company unfortunately shut down after failing to gain enough capital to survive.

The market for dating apps is extremely competitive, with a high volume of new brands trying to compete; it is estimated that over 90 percent of startups in the dating app industry fail. It was unfortunate a company like Siren couldn't work out because it was an app designed to protect and empower women. The good news is a dating app called Bumble, which operates in a similar fashion, is now the second largest dating app next to Tinder.

This app, which does use the swipe option, only allows women to initiate the conversation after both her and the desired partner swipe right. By allowing women to start the conversation, she has the power to dictate the conversation and choose whether or not this person is worth her time. Just because this is centered around the female making the first move does not mean the app is anti-male. In my talks with men who have used the app in the past, they mention that the app is, in fact, somewhat of a relief in that when a woman messages them, there is clear-cut communication already being established in terms of romantic interest with consent.

---

6   Leanna Garfield, "What it's like to use Siren, the new dating app that aims to be classier than Tinder," *Business Insider*, October 17, 2016.

7   Taylor Soper, "Dating app Siren, which empowered women, shuts down after running out of money," *Geek Wire*, April 5, 2017.

Iliana Vazuka, who will be also mentioned in later chapters, found her current boyfriend via Bumble. At the time, she was new to dating apps and was extremely skeptical. She said her mindset as a new user on Bumble was, *"whether or not it works out, at least you had a new experience by meeting someone new. Who knows, you could possibly meet a close friend!"* Iliana was truthful to herself in what she was looking for. Her advice to people entering the dating world, whether it be in-person or via an app, was to simply *"be honest with what you want because in doing so, you will find someone who will help you mature and grow as a person."*

Unlike the dating apps mentioned above, The League is, quite literally, in a league of its own. For better or for worse, this app is a superficial dating platform for the well-educated and the wealthy. How is this so? To be on the app, you must first apply and then will automatically be placed on their waiting list. The purpose of the waiting list is so the app's administrators can determine whether your profile is "worthy enough" through social status (based on higher education and income). Depending on the city you live in, the waiting list can be over forty thousand people long. Places like New York, DC, and Chicago typically have longer waiting lists because more people have signed up for the app. There is a way, however, to accelerate the process by paying a non-refundable $300 initiation fee to have your profile looked at and approved by what they call "a concierge."

Because of the unusual, yet strict, screening process of each profile (must be connected with both LinkedIn and Facebook along with submitting six photographs of yourself), The League rarely experiences catfish accounts or fake profiles like Tinder or Bumble. A friend of mine Matthew Redmond, who currently works at an investment bank in Delaware, was one of the first users of the app. He told me:

"I've only been on one date through the app. But that date led to a brief relationship. Since then, I have used the app on and off. What I like about it is there is surprisingly a lot of women in my area who use the app."

Dating apps have enhanced the way we date which I think is to our benefit overall. Out of all of the dating apps mentioned and others including OkCupid, Hinge, and Happn, the women I know and have interviewed tend to gravitate toward Bumble. This does not mean every woman loves Bumble, but Bumble seems to be the preferred app for those who are looking for something serious.

Social media messaging is another major asset; personally, this has been the most successful in cultivating long-term romantic connections. Reconnecting or establishing a connection with new people via Facebook can be a healthy alternative to dating digitally. Facebook has even introduced its own dating service. The Facebook dating feature operates as an app within an app. Only your name and age will be displayed, and you can upload up to nine photos. There are a series of questions you can answer to help spark conversation with other users. Sharing details of your hobbies, interests, and location are the primary methods of finding potential dates. Facebook dating feature users can directly message profiles they like without waiting for the other profile to like them back.

Other social media outlets such as Twitter can also be utilized to find the love of your life. For example, my friend Hector Rivera told me he and his wife met via Twitter. He said, "*it started out through just retweeting our posts, then eventually we decided that we wanted to meet up.*" His wife and daughter currently reside in Puerto Rico while Hector lives here in DC. He and his wife communicate via phone and Skype and, when the opportunity arises, he will either fly out to Puerto Rico or they will fly in to DC.

Putting unnecessary pressure on ourselves to find someone immediately can be a detriment to our overall well-being and mental health. Some studies have shown excessive use of dating apps have led to increased feelings of loneliness and depression. The peer-reviewed journal *Body Image* published a 2017 study on the effects of dating apps and self-esteem. The study suggested "*about 1,300 (mostly) college-age students were asked about their Tinder use, body image and self-esteem. The study found that men and women who use the app appear to have lower self-esteem than those who don't. In general, Tinder users reported less satisfaction with their bodies and looks than non-users.*"[8]

Jessica Strübel, who authored the study, mentions, "*as a result of how the app works and what it requires of its users, people who are on Tinder after a while may begin to feel depersonalized and disposable in their social interactions, develop heightened awareness (and criticism) of their looks and bodies and believe that there is always something better around the*

8   Juliet Marateck, "Online dating lowers self-esteem and increases depression, studies say," *CNN.com*, May 29, 2018.

corner, or rather with the next swipe of their screen, even while
questioning their own worth."[8]

Much like social media, dating apps can be great for logistical purposes and finding new people with only the power of a swipe. The problem is you cannot gauge a person purely from their pictures. If a picture says a thousand words, a personality says a million.

RECOMMENDATION:
Try to think of dating apps as more of a tool than a complete replacement for organic in-person dating. These apps are designed for you to meet new people you otherwise may not have interacted with or have access to organically. Using this tool in moderation can be beneficial to your life, but it is not worth getting too stressed out over any lack of success from an app. Take any "bad experiences" as learning experiences. You also don't have to pressure yourself into finding a perfect match immediately. It will take time. Enjoy the process, whether or not it involves dating apps, and be kind to yourself along the way.

CHAPTER 3

THE FUTURE OF DATING

——

As technology advances, so will the way we socialize and interact with each other. Dating apps have made substantial progress over the past decade. From the year 2000 until now, there has been an explosion of new and unique dating services. If we want to look at the future, we might need to look at other countries that are already advancing in this direction.

Julie Austin of the World Future Society writes:[9]

> *"In order to predict the future, you need to see the big picture, which includes the past and other cultures and countries. As a futurist and innovator I believe history repeats itself, but in a new and innovative way that integrates new technology with old traditions. In many countries there is the tradition of arranged marriages, where family and friends choose your mate based on economics, class and religion. It's accepted that family and friends know best about who would be a perfect match. That's not such a*

——

9   Quinn Myers, "Futurists Predict What Online Dating Will Look Like in 10 years," *Melmagazine*, December 11, 2018.

stretch when you think that those are the people who know you best and want the best for you."

To further understand the future of dating we will look at Japan, which has had to combat a serious problem with its citizens experiencing higher levels of loneliness. In 2017, Bloomberg did a story on single Japanese citizens beginning to resort to virtual reality as a way to medicate their void of romance and intimacy. According to the National Institute of Population and Social Security Research of Japan, "*70 percent of unmarried men and 60 percent of unmarried women aged eighteen to thirty-four have not had a relationship with the opposite sex.*"[10]

Minori Takechi is the CEO of Gatebox, a company that creates virtual reality experiences. The company's product can give the emotional connection the same way a human can through a hologram-like experience. The hologram, which the company is experimenting with, is a female character named Hikori Azuma. CEO Takechi refers to the hologram as "*the wife of the future. She can wake you up in the morning and welcome you home. When it gets late, she might suggest going to bed.*"[10]

The product can also be linked to any smartphone, which would allow for the device to send you personal messages similar to what a real-life companion might say. Examples may look like the following: "When are you coming home?," "Will you be late to dinner?," and "I miss you."

---

10   *Bloomberg Quick Take Originals.* "Japan, Virtual Partners Fill Romantic Void," September 22, 2017, video, 1:03.

In 2017, the company launched its prototype with over three hundred orders placed at a price tag of $2,700 per unit.10 It may take a while for the western world to use holograms to temporarily replace real relationships, but this seems highly unlikely (at least for now). The use of artificial intelligence (AI) in dating, however, is a reality not too far off. Some companies and start-ups within the dating app industry are beginning to experiment with this technology.

Artificial intelligence will not be used as a tool to replace human intimacy, but rather the purpose of incorporating AI will be to better categorize and specify potential partners who fit our desired criteria. CEO of Match Group Mandy Ginsberg says AI *"will put more people in front of you that you are more likely to say yes to."*[11]

One of the first dating applications to use artificial intelligence is an app called Quinn. The app limits you to just five people; their perspective target market, according to the company's co-founder Dan Joyce, is *"genuine relationship seekers"* who are in their late twenties to thirties. The next trend in dating, according to Joyce, is *"curation and person-alization fueled by artificial intelligence."* [11]

As stated earlier, the digital dating climate is continuing to evolve rapidly; Ginsberg mentions, *"ten years ago, 3 percent of relationships started with an app. Today it's over 30 per-ceent."*[11] The stigma of online dating is also continuing to change towards a more positive direction, making it more

---

11   *Marketwatch*, How AI and video could transform the online dating industry," May 4, 2018, video, 1:24.

culturally acceptable. Users who are invested in the dating scene typically use more than one dating app. Currently, dating apps use photos as a form of reconnaissance before setting up in-person dates. Dating in the future will begin to incorporate much more video interaction. Think of the evolution of social media from Facebook and Instagram to TikTok. Video interaction allows users to hear the voices, personality traits, and sense of humor, which are otherwise hard to discover through only a photo or messaging. First dates will look entirely different, becoming more virtual than being randomly set up at a coffee shop.

As we've witnessed as a result of the coronavirus pandemic, the complete and sudden switch to virtual learning and professional workspace is already forcing us to change how we socialize. Virtual happy hours, birthday parties, and even dating are now becoming part of the norm which otherwise would have seemed odd only a couple months ago. Being forced to adapt was difficult in the beginning, but now people are adapting to this alternative form of communication and access. Virtual dates are not as odd as they may appear and have become commonplace given the realities of the coronavirus pandemic.

Imperial College Business School and eharmony in the UK teamed up to develop a study that predicted what dating would look like by the year 2040. The report suggests matchmaking services in the future will include "*full-sensory virtual dating, biotechnology, behavior-based matching, and artificial intelligence.*"[12] Data will also be able to match and simulate all five of the human senses, allowing the app to digitally create *"a full-sensory virtual reality"* experience. With this technology, participants will be able to simulate holding hands or even smelling a fragrance, all within the comfort of your own living room. This means a participant could essentially go on a real date without having met the person face to face. Similar to the hologram experiment by Gatebox in Japan, virtual reality will serve as an alternative for those who want to meet their needs for physical intimacy yet can't find it in the real world.

This also means a participant could feel like they are going on a real date without having met the person face-to-face. On a more relatable note, there are advantages for couples who are in long-distance relationships. Rather than relying on phone or video calls, virtual reality could help create the sensation that their long-distance partner is still physically with them.

Behavior-based matching and artificial intelligence are the most practical and more realistic outcomes of what will happen in the future of dating. Behavior-based match making would get rid of surveys and questionnaires and instead utilize online behavioral tracking to monitor your live reaction to a person by tracking your heart rate, neural signals in the brain, and even facial recognition. Computer algorithms will be able to generate potential partners based on these responses.[12] Artificial intelligence, much like how it is used

---

12 Imperial College Business School, "The Future of Dating 2040," *eHarmony*, published November 2015.

today, will use machine learning to help influence your decisions when trying to find a long-term mate.

Lastly, the report indicates virtual reality can help prepare us for practice dates. This technology can help those who are nervous or anxious before a date by going through a practice simulation before the date begins. A simulation, I think, is actually not a bad idea. It can be nerve wracking trying to start and maintain conversations as the night goes on without practice. From my own experience, even with extensive conversational practice with book interviews and podcasts, staying sharp beforehand is essential no matter the occasion.

Host of the *Brain Games* Jason Silva said this in an interview with *MEL Magazine*:[9]

> *"I think one of the double-edged swords of technology is that it floods us with new options—so over the next decade, it will be easier than ever to meet someone new, but by the same token, harder than ever to hold our attention on that person.*
>
> *The paralysis of choice will be overwhelming. Perhaps monogamous committed relationships will be called into question, simply because our brains will be overwhelmed with mate choice. I also think advances in artificial intelligence will provide us with the option of dating 'virtual people' online, similar to the movie Her, and for many this will suffice."*[9]

The view on dating is changing and we've seen some countries becoming more desperate than others in terms of partnering its citizens. In the US, dating seems to have an abundant amount of resources that allow people to find that special someone. In other countries, however, there is a different narrative being played.

Founder of Futurist.com Glen Hiemstra stated:[9]

> "We can note that many countries (Sweden, Japan, etc.) are concerned about the lack of dating and coupling in a declining-population scenario. And we can also note that there are reports in the US that young people are less sexually active than in earlier history.
>
> That must be a combination of delayed marriage and the impact of the online world on the analog (dating) world. While people continue to use online dating apps as a way to meet—and many relationships start there—perhaps it does not work as often.
>
> Changing cultural standards about how women are to be treated is another significant factor. As is gender fluidity. Both are changing how we view the old concept of dating. The future is supposed to be characterized by more use of AI in dating apps to provide better matches, and that could lead to more significant relationships earlier. The challenge for young people will, as always, be one of finding ways to meet once one is out of school or other settings where lots of young people gather."

If we take a look at patterns in the current age, companies such as Amazon, Uber, and Grubhub are highly successful because of the following common denominators: quicker delivery and reliability. I believe this same approach will be applied to dating. As we search for ways to become more comfortable and exert less energy on the essentials, virtual reality and artificial intelligence will be next in line to make our need for intimacy a much more instantaneous experience.

Clinical sexologist and psychotherapist Kristie Overstreet claims, *"in the next few years, dating is going to be extremely individualized. We're going to hone in on our preferences, from looks to location, just like we do when ordering food. That doesn't guarantee happily ever after, but it does give you a good shot at it because you'll be able to weed out people more quickly."*[13]

As we've seen how the stigma has evolved through dating apps, we should have an open mind when these kinds of technologies are introduced to us. Some of this may seem scary to read about at first, same as the concept of social media would have been unfamiliar to those living in the eighties and nineties. But who knows, these new technologies might become the new norm. For example, experts predict that by the year 2024, AI will be so far advanced we may no longer have language barriers when trying to date people outside of our culture. Imagine being able to date someone from Italy, France, or China without any language barrier.[11]

In a way, we don't really have a choice in terms of preventing new technologies from developing. What we do have control

---

13   Julie Vadnal, "The Future of Dating: Where Relationships Are Heading," *Bumble,* 2020.

of, however, are our actions and doing what's best for our own mental and physical health.

CHAPTER 4

SOCIAL PRESSURES TO BE IN A RELATIONSHIP

———

Any potential romantic interest who doesn't share the same feelings of intimacy as you does not reflect your potential. It could be they are just not into you right now or they have a different set of criteria for a partner—don't take it personally. Everyone has different desires and preferences, which is why it is important to be honest with yourself and respect their decision.

People go through many major transitions in their lives and perhaps, through their perspective, you might not be a part of that transition, at least not yet. Our interests transform from our early twenties to mid-thirties. It is okay to say you are just looking for hookups and not anything serious. No one's opinion matters except yours because you are the one living your life.

The world, however, can be unforgiving and pressure you to find that special someone quicker than you plan. Especially as we get older, family and friends will pose questions such as: "When are you getting married?" and "When are you having kids?" They may not intend to come across that way, but this may subconsciously add more pressure to what you have already put on yourself.

According to a 2015 study performed by the American Sociological Association called "Who Wants the Breakup? Gender and Breakup in Heterosexual Couples," out of the 2,262 adults surveyed (ages nineteen to ninety-four), 371 of those adults had broken up or were in the process of getting a divorce. In an analysis conducted by Michael Rosenfeld, who is a sociology professor from Stanford University, he indicated *"women initiated 69 percent of all divorces, compared to 31 percent for men."*[14] Regardless, if the relationship was a marriage or non-marital, women initiated the breakup at a similar rate. Rosenfeld states, *"women seem to have a predominant role in initiating divorces in the US as far back as there is data from a variety of sources, back to the 1940s."*[14]

Rosenfeld continues to explain, *"marriage as an institution has been a little bit slow to catch up with the expectations for gender equality. Wives still take their husbands' surnames, and are sometimes pressured to do so. Husbands still expect their wives to do the bulk of the housework and the bulk of the childcare. On the other hand, I think that non-marital relationships lack the historical baggage and*

---

14   Michael Rosenfeld, "Who wants the Breakup? Gender and Breakup in Heterosexual Couples," *Stanford,* published 2017.

expectations of marriage, which makes the non-marital relationships more flexible and more adaptable to modern expectations, including women's expectations for more gender equality."[14]

Since 2005, Professor Kerry Cronin from Boston College has been offering her students extra credit for going on dates with each other. In order for a student to receive credit on the "dating assignment," they needed to follow a set of guidelines which included the act of asking out another classmate in person, a date must last between sixty and ninety minutes, meals must not exceed $10 (to indicate this is not serious), no physical engagement outside of a hug, have three to four questions prepared, "you ask you pay," and no alcohol or drug use. Cronin claims going out to dinner on a first date is not a good idea, as the situation becomes *"overly serious where the stakes are too high."*[15]

The hardest part of the assignment, according to students, was battling through the awkwardness of asking someone out. This is a counter-cultural act for those in their early twenties because they are used to digital interactions that allow for technology to do the hard work via matchmaking algorithms. Are the scripts in our current dating culture lost? Does effort correlate to success in the dating world? There seems to be a battle between the desire to meet physical urges versus finding intimacy.

15   *EWTN.* "World Over-2018-04-12- 'The Dating Project,' Dr. Kerry Cronin with Raymond Arroyo," April 13, 2018, video 9:12.

Environments can especially shape the pressures of needing to be in a relationship as soon as possible. Rushing the process can be detrimental for any person trying to find a mate, as they could find the wrong person for them.

Sometimes it is understandable why friends and family may feel concerned their son or daughter has not settled down especially, after reaching thirty. However, it is important to show support and not make young people feel pressured into signing up for a situation they may not be ready for.

Proximity is another important variable that may add pressure to you getting into a relationship. Social media might say you have over one thousand followers or friends but, in reality, you may only have a close few you keep in frequent contact with. Within that circle, research shows you may be more attracted to those inside your circle than out. This is because you have a more intimate understanding of that person, unlike a stranger who may fit your physical desires but who you don't know deep down. Proximity within a social group may heighten the pressure of forming a romantic relationship with someone internally, especially if the group strongly encourages it.

Proximity can also play a role in forcing couples to stay together. Social pressures, as well as family and sharing the same friends, make it more difficult for a couple to break up because they don't want to disappoint the people closest to them. Especially if a partner gets along well with parents or other close family members, it may result in the couple's relationship lasting longer which does more harm than good to the relationship. **Sometimes breaking up when the time** is right is better than waiting or delaying the inevitable, which could result in negative and sometimes devastating outcomes for both parties.

Pressure can essentially arise in all forms, but the argument here is pressure from external forces should *not* be a key factor in either staying in or ending the relationship.

Jenna Ryu, a senior at Georgetown University and the girlfriend of my fraternity brother, already has a unique yet adventurous background. She has traveled internationally and has lived in four different states in the US. Jenna was open about what she has learned about herself thus far; I believe her advice developed from her dating experiences is sound and people, especially at my age, need to hear it:

"It's never a good idea to blindly plan your future around someone else. Looking too far into the future can feel exciting, however, the present is also unexpected which is why we need to enjoy what's right in front of us.

You have to love yourself before you love someone because if you don't love yourself, you could end up in a toxic situation with a partner who doesn't treat you right."

Jenna is a firm believer in the theory of self-love, while also continuing to focus on her professional career. She excels in journalism and has aspirations to one day pursue a PhD specializing in clinical psychology.

Focusing on education, career choice, and a need to establish yourself are important aspects of life that need to be strongly considered before placing pressure on yourself to find the love of your life. Only enter a relationship if you feel you have developed yourself to some capacity (either personally or professionally). Becoming a person who is self-sustainable and who knows what you want will make you a happier partner to be around with in the long term. **Be open and honest with what you want**; only you know what's truly best for you.

I asked my friend Alexis (from the earlier chapter) for some advice she might have for millennials looking to settle down and start a family. She told me:

"My advice to millennials who are ready to start a family would be to try your best to be prepared, but there is never going to be a right moment. The most important thing is to make sure the relationship is strong and both people are equally invested because parenthood is all about teamwork. Becoming a parent should never be one-sided and the effort should be equally distributed.

Marriage versus single life is about working together and merging two lives into one. It's not just you anymore when you marry the right person. It's a beautiful thing. With every good thing comes sacrifice and understanding, but the reward is so worth it."

Exercises in **emotional intelligence** can especially help you to further understand yourself and what makes you tick. Dating is not black and white because each person is unique and will play a unique role in your life, whether it is long-term or short-term. Emotional intelligence is not taught in school, and it can help strengthen your decision making by asking yourself the following questions:[16]

1) *Who do you want to be?*

_____

2) *Who are you now?*

_____

3) *How do you get from here to there?*

_____

4) *How do you make change stick?*

_____

5) *Who can help you?*

_____

---

16 Daniel Goleman, Richard Boyateis, and Anne Mckee, "*On Emotional Intelligence: Primal Leadership*," (Boston: Harvard Business Review Press, 2015), 26-27.

PART II

PRINCIPLES
OF SELF-LOVE

CHAPTER 5

LOVE YOURSELF FIRST

———

Being happy is not a forever state. It is simply not realistic nor is it healthy to suppress other emotions such as sadness, anger, nervousness, or anxiety. Embracing those other emotions is the key to managing your mental and physical health. The point of this chapter is to give you some tips on how to lift your mood within a short period of time. Just remember to *give yourself permission to be human!*

The journey toward loving yourself begins only once you accept and take ownership of the way you feel. This may include changing your personal habits, work environment, social circles, and even relationships with family members.

The opposite of happiness is not "feeling unhappy" but rather "apathy," which is the loss of joy, enthusiasm, and passion. Some people may be overly pessimistic toward your goals or ambitions and are not the kind of people you want to surround yourself with. It is okay to have people around with conflicting viewpoints, but only entertain their suggestions to a certain degree where it's not toxic to your own health.

Why is it that we might feel like we need to achieve certain goals in life in order to be happy? Why does being happy sometimes seem like a faraway destination? Well, happiness is not something you necessarily achieve or are awarded because of accomplishing something. Being happy is simply loving yourself, your family, and your friends; you can literally be happy about anything! You can feel happy simply by listening to music or getting comfortable on the couch. There are all kinds of aspects in life that can make us happy but, most importantly, happiness comes from within us—it's a decision to let a good feeling continue.

Martin Seligman, director of the Penn Positive Psychology Center at the University of Pennsylvania, was one of the first psychologists to introduce the concept of positive psychology into mainstream consciousness. In a TED Talk from 2008, Dr. Seligman discussed the three types of "**Happy Lives**": [17]

1) **The Pleasant Life:** Having as many pleasures as possible, mostly pertaining to materials. There are two major setbacks when pursuing this kind of lifestyle, which include the fact that it's *"heritable and habituates."*
2) **Life of Engagement:** Work—love—play. Combining the raw feeling of pleasure versus flow. When in a flow state, you can't feel anything, yet you know it's happening.
3) **The Meaningful Life:** This involves knowing your highest strengths and using it to better serve a larger mission or purpose.[17]

---

17   *TED,* "Martin Seligman: The new era of positive psychology," July 21, 2008, video, 9:34.

Former professor Tal Ben-Shahar taught an experimental class at Harvard related to the pursuit of happiness. The class was called Intro to Positive Psychology. Word quickly spread and this once-experimental class would become the most popular class at Harvard at the time. Author Shawn Achor was a disciple of Tal Ben-Shahar's teachings in positive psychology and wrote his own book called *The Happiness Advantage: The Seven Principles of Positive Psychology That Fuel Success and Performance at Work.*

In his book, Achor tackles the notion many of us may have been taught: only when you work hard will you'll become successful, and once you are successful, then you'll be happy. Positive psychology dislocates this idea by theorizing that *"our brains work in the opposite way. **Happiness actually fuels success**, not the other way around."* [18]

Achor writes:[18]

> *"Every time we are successful, we merely move the goal posts of what success looks like. If happiness is on the opposite side of success, every time you change what success looks like happiness gets pushed over the horizon.*

---

18   Shawn Achor, "*The Happiness Advantage*" (New York: Crown, 2010), 3.

If you can find a way to get your brain to become positive, your success rate will increase and, as a result, work will become more productive, enjoyable and rewarding."

Now I understand certain aspects of life can hurt and feel extremely negative. That's something unavoidable, which makes being a state of happiness a major challenge. No matter who you are, I can guarantee you have faced some hardships, have had people give you negative feedback about yourself, or even had someone close to you disappoint or betray your trust. The point is we all have to move on from those negative experiences and focus on our own self-worth to better the lives of our future family.

To help elevate your state of self-happiness, I strongly suggest you try to implement the following exercises which have helped me tremendously in times when I needed to build positive momentum:

1) **Express Gratitude:** You can do this by writing in a journal or on a piece of paper stating three to five things you are grateful for. On the subject of journaling, this is a great way to organize your thoughts and outline your own call to action. I was personally not into journaling until recently. It has been a major help in allowing the flow of ideas, relaxing my mental state, and developing my plans for the future.

2) **Get Physically Active**: Any kind of physical activity can contribute significantly to your state of happiness, yet the most common excuse for not exercising is lack of time. The best way to combat this is to simply admit time is not the enemy. Another reason we might choose not to exercise is we are afraid of devoting that amount of energy when that energy could be spent on other important areas in our lives. From my own experience, exercising has helped me get back my self-confidence. My exercise of choice is Muay Thai kickboxing, which allows me to break away from the parts of life that stress me out.

3) **Read**: When I was younger, I did not like reading because I associated reading with schoolwork. Now that I'm older, reading has played a huge role in my level of happiness. Reading for me feels like exercise for the brain and spirit. The more I read, the more I began to learn about myself.

4) **Be Kind**: Performing an act of kindness can truly bring feelings of fulfillment and connection. Since entering college, giving back has been a truly humbling experience I'm proud of. The feeling of helping others is everlasting, which can inspire others to help the cause.

It is important to remember you are not going to have all the time in the world to take care of yourself first. Once you get married and start a family, it may become increasingly challenging to take care of your interests as other priorities and responsibilities begin to emerge.

In this next section, we'll be talking about perseverance and love. The following two people I interviewed are close friends who have experienced life's harshest realities, yet still exemplify what it means to be caring and loving individuals.

First is Iliana Vazuka, who was mentioned earlier in the chapter about dating apps. Iliana lost her father while she was in college. He was a brilliant electrical engineer who played the role of stay-at-home dad to take care of his daughters. He, at one point, had to choose between family and career, but he chose family. Even though he had to sacrifice his own professional ambitions, becoming closer to his family gave him a true sense of belonging and he was able to provide for and love each of his daughters unconditionally.

Iliana explains that it was *"beneficial to have someone who could show you how you should be treated. He was the best person I ever met. I wouldn't be who I am today if it wasn't for him. Unfortunately, he hasn't seen who I've become. He's not going to walk me down the aisle. He isn't going to meet any of my children. There are so many aspects of my life that he is not going to experience. I can imagine that he'll be proud of me, although I won't hear those words from him. It is surreal to lose someone so pivotal in your life, someone who has helped shape you."*

I was impressed by how much her father influenced her yet, despite losing such a pivotal piece in her life, she still remains positive and maintains the motivation fueling her success. What I learned after talking with Iliana is we need to replenish our souls by surrounding ourselves with people who give us unconditional love and support. Words not only matter but can move the mountains in your own life. Iliana emphasizes the importance of *"celebrating the little victories in life,"* which has helped propel her career. She was recently accepted into the prestigious Chicago Booth School of Business and will be attending next fall.

Next up is David Daniel Cooper, another close friend and former teammate from my football and lacrosse teams. He is an aspiring musician and business student at George Mason University. Having known David for so many years, he is one of the strongest men in my life. I've watched him lose so much yet he still continues to stay disciplined and pursue his dreams. I asked him about what makes him happy, his personal life lessons, and how he overcomes obstacles in the real world.

David explains:

> "What I've learned about myself over the past few years is that I can bend, but I'll never break. I've experienced quite a bit of heartache and pain in my late twenties and throughout most of my life. I've lost family and friends to suicide, drug addiction, cancer, and even what some may call an act of God. I've been told by many of my friends I'm one of the strongest people they've ever met but, behind closed doors, that hasn't always been the case. I've spiraled into deep depression and I've struggled with mental illness constantly.

> There have been days where it has seemed like it's all too much, but I've never given up hope. I've found healthy ways to cope through meditation, reading, writing, exercise, and other positive channels. I'll always fight to stay strong

mentally, physically, and emotionally. Not only for myself, but for the ones who love and support me as well."

What self-happiness means to me is loving and learning about yourself every day. It's about discovering what inspires you and what makes you tick. It's getting out of your comfort zone and experiencing things you never even dreamed you would. It's setting aside time for self-care and enjoying the small blessings life has to offer."

Typically, we may think happiness as something achieved by reaching a certain goal or waiting for that special moment. *The truth is we need to be happy with what we have now in order to enjoy those special moments in the future.*

If you wait for the future to make yourself happy, all that will happen is you will become more depressed when those moments take longer to arrive. Life is not easy, and you will continue to stumble upon obstacles that will seem challenging. The benefit of being happy is you will be more successful on the days you might have felt lazy. You will have more strength on days you might have otherwise felt weak. Finally, you will have more passion and excitement in your life which will help improve the lives of those closest to you.

CHAPTER 6

MAXIMIZE YOUR CALENDAR

———

Taking care of your calendar means taking steps toward your dreams. The way you manage your time is the key determinant in whether or not you will achieve your goals, as well as making time for activities that make you happy. So how does this relate to relationships? Managing your time is how you achieve balance in your life. Without balance, there is no way you will be able to maintain a healthy relationship with another person. Much like the example used in the beginning of this book, you need to put your oxygen mask on first before helping someone else.

Harvard psychologist Matt Killingsworth and his colleague Mihaly Csikzentmihalyi conducted a study on how happiness and time management intersect with each other:[19]

---

19   Francis Wade, "Can Happiness Be Created With Proper Time Management?" *Lifehack,* accessed 2020.

*"**We are happiest (and most productive) when we are able to enter the flow state**—an ecstatic experience of total concentration that requires our complete attention due to its difficulty. We found that this is more likely to happen when we are at the office: we often derive more enjoyment from work than from time off, due to the fact that we feel skillful, and challenged, and therefore feel more happy, strong, creative and satisfied.*

It's not because work is inherently better, but it is well-structured. It appears that we are confused about what real happiness is and what it looks like from one moment to the next. We tell ourselves that we'll be happy when we win the lottery, not understanding that after the money is in the bank, we'll be just as unhappy as before if we allow our minds to wander.

Forty-seven percent of the time, people are thinking about something other than what they're currently doing. Consider that statistic next time you're sitting in a meeting or driving down the street."

The great thing is "**loving your calendar**" is much easier than it appears to be. It simply takes some alone time. Here are some quick tips to help you manage your calendar more effectively.

10 WAYS TO HELP ORGANIZE YOUR TIME:

1. **Meditate**: This can include closing your eyes or writing down your thoughts on any piece of paper. I highly recommend you **turn off your phone** while you do this. Especially with social media apps, our brains can become wired to constantly check our phones which can disrupt our ability to focus.

2. **Begin with a simple cleaning**: Whether it be your bedroom, workplace, or even your car, getting rid of clutter will not only help organize your physical space, but will allow you to execute the next step with a clear state of mind.

3. **Write down your goals for the week**: The purpose of goal setting is to help you keep track of whether or not you are accomplishing your priorities. By clearly articulating these goals, you are more likely to get it done. Research shows once you write down a goal, you are 80 percent more likely to complete it.

4. **Spend time doing your most important tasks first**: Try to avoid saving it for later. Award-winning actor Denzel Washington once said in a speech that *"ease is the enemy to progress."* By doing the hardest tasks first you will have conquered your responsibilities, rather than saving it for later and being more stressed in the long-term.

5. **Take frequent breaks while engaging in difficult tasks**: When you are first starting out, especially if it's a difficult project, don't pressure yourself into sitting down for three hours at a time. Be patient with yourself and take intermittent breaks to refocus.

6. **Schedule specific times for replying (emails/social media)**: On a more realistic level, if you are engaged in social media like I am it can be extremely difficult

to put the phone down. By scheduling reply times, you will essentially be rewarding yourself by giving yourself breaks rather than checking your phone constantly. Scheduling blocks of time will allow you to get more done in a shorter time frame.

7. **Search for inspiration**: When you feel mentally drained or have reached a plateau in your progress, step away from your work and take time to search for something that inspires you (e.g., podcasts, music, TED Talks).

8. **Begin to audit your days**: This means looking at specific times where there may be a large gap in down time. Start by writing down your actions throughout the day, then see how you can better utilize those open blocks of time in the future.

9. **Find a mentor**: A mentor can help keep you accountable. They will also guide you and introduce you to their network of people. Mentorship can help propel you in the right direction.

10. **Practice is making progress**: If you struggle with time management, be patient because it will take time to fully develop a new routine. But by taking it one day at a time and journaling your progress, you will eventually live your desired lifestyle. Find what works best for you, continue to make adjustments, and love the journey to becoming your best self. In my opinion, **progress is the key to happiness**.

What I've learned is people who are happier in their relationships manage their time well. Even though we all have twenty-four hours in a day, we may not have full control over our time, especially if we have a family to take care of. The list mentioned above details tasks that will not take much of your time.

Try not to overwhelm yourself with too many activities all at once. Doing so may further dissuade you from taking action. **Momentum** is a huge part of taking back control of your life. The more you continue to do activities you want to do, the more confident you'll become in trusting yourself. Transformation occurs in incremental steps.

> *Enjoy the journey of change** and try not to get too caught up in reaching that "final destination."

Just remember you have the ability to move mountains, but it will require patience and perseverance for that to happen.

Looking at the latest research, this is how some of the world's top CEO's maximize their time. The reason we want to focus on CEOs is because a majority of them still maintain a stable life despite having fully committed schedules. Their vision for both themselves and their companies must match their schedules.

Derived from the book *The CEO Next Door* by Elena Botelho and Kim Powell, here are ways highly reliable CEOs balance their time while taking care of their own actions:[20]

---

20 Kim Powell, R. Powell and Elena L. Botelho, *The CEO Next Door*," (New York: Currency Publishing, 2018), 69.

- *They are on time for meetings, for planes, for phone calls*
- *They make individual commitments (who is taking what actions when) clear in meetings*
- *They follow up on agreed-upon actions religiously*
- *They make lists (to do, to read, mistakes, people to keep in touch with, useful resources, etc.) and put those lists into action*
- *They are aware of their mood, words, actions, and in their interactions with their teams— are their actions and words having the desired effects?*
- *They keep the people who need to know in the loop so no one drops the ball*

At the end of this book, there is a **30-DAY SELF-LOVE PLAN** to help you map out your most important activities, events, and social activities.

There is an opportunity cost to every aspect of life. Your responsibility is to figure out which activity or plan of action is best suited for you. Being able to maximize your time will require time! Be patient with yourself and simply make small improvements every day. It may not seem like much in the beginning, but eventually your incremental progress will transform itself into a building of your success. Don't forget to stay positive along the way!

CHAPTER 7

THE POWER OF EMPATHY AND GIVING BACK

———

Abigail Marsh was nineteen years old when she almost lost her life. She was driving back home on the highway when suddenly a dog dashed across the road and almost collided with her car. She instinctively swerved to avoid a collision, which resulted in her car being cemented in the speed lane of the highway. A male stranger pulled his car over and miraculously ran across five lanes of oncoming highway traffic to help rescue her. [21] She never got the chance to see him again, but to this day gives him a generous and a loving thank you every time she gives a speech.

What sparks these kinds of good deeds in people? A stranger risked his life for no reward, social applause, or television

———

21   Abigail Marsh, *"Fear Factor* "(New York: Basic Books, 2017), 2.

recognition; he simply acted without hesitation to save someone else's life.

Abigail Marsh is the author of the book *Fear Factor*, and her TED Talk on altruism has reached over two million views on the official TED Talk website. She is currently a professor at Georgetown University and happens to be my former professor from the spring 2018 semester. The class she taught was called Empathy and Communication within the Psychology Department.

The class had a practical approach in teaching students how to empathize and see different perspectives. I remember around the second or third week of class, we began discussing a case study. We were paired up with a person who shared a contradicting opinion. My partner was a senior at the time, and we disagreed heavily on the subject. However, we would both eventually discover that, despite having a difference in opinion on one subject, we did in fact share a ton of other common personality traits. We would later become friends and hang out at Tombs (local Georgetown bar) at least once a week.

What I learned about myself was I could become friends with someone despite different opinions. He was able to empathize with some of the racism I experienced as a child, which connected us on a much deeper level.

In an interview earlier this year, Professor Marsh discussed with me the importance of not subscribing to personal bias. She explains: "*I hate boiling people down to group membership. One person is not a reflection of their entire group.*" I also brought up the topic of toxic masculinity and whether it is a real problem for the reputation of men. She reassured me *"toxic masculinity is not a reflection of all men, just as no trait applies to all members of any group."* In fact, characteristics such as *"heroic and wonderful"* should also be placed in the conversation. Professor Marsh is currently married; her husband is a former US Marine and they have two lovely daughters.

What I learned from not only taking her class but also interviewing her is that blindly labeling or characterizing any group of people because of one person's reputation is an unfair method for judging character.

Acts of altruism, according to Professor Marsh, can be defined as *"a voluntary, costly behavior with the goal of improving another's welfare."*[21] Acts of altruism can come in a variety of forms, such as giving to the homeless, food donations, putting your life at risk to save another through search and rescue, and kidney donations, and it is a discipline Professor Marsh focuses much of her research on.

On the topic of empathy, billionaire hedge fund manager, and philanthropist Ray Dalio discusses in his book *Principles* how becoming an empathetic leader helped position his companies towards a successful trajectory.

Dalio states, *"empathetic people are superb at recognizing and meeting the needs of clients, customers, or subordinates. They seem approachable, wanting to hear what people have to say.*

They listen carefully, picking up on what people are truly concerned about, and they respond on the mark."[22]

It is vital we take time to combat our own egos. Internal conflicts are even shown within the brain, where the prefrontal cortex goes up against the amygdala (the part of the brain responsible for empathy).

Recognizing how your ego works will help you not only deal with external conflict but will also help you make better and clearer decisions. For example, if someone disagrees with you then it may feel like a natural reaction to respond with anger. In this state of mind, logic is absent and so is reasoning; *"if you are too proud of what you know or of how good you are at something you will learn less, make inferior decisions, and fall short of your potential."*[22]

Understanding your greatest weakness involves one of the most important character traits in any successful leader: **humility**. Dalio writes, *"humility can be even more valuable than having good mental maps if it leads you to seek out better answers than you could come up with on your own. Having both open-mindedness and good mental maps is most powerful of all."*[22]

There is a major difference between pride and aspiration. Pride is when the ego pollutes your conscience, thereby giving you a false sense of power. Aspiration (in healthy doses) allows you to build yourself into the person you wish to become. You don't have to wait until the new year to be the

---

22 Ray Dalio, *"Principles"* (New York: Simon & Schuster, 2017), 180.

"new you," you can transform yourself at any time. First, it takes reflection—you truly need to understand how you tick before you can fix anything. Journaling is a powerful tool that can help uncover how you really feel and what kinds of triggers you may have.

Sometimes the concept of self-love can be misconstrued with being selfish. The point of loving yourself simply means taking care of yourself first before making others happy. To put it plain and simple, this is the healthiest way to live a happy life. By taking care of yourself first, you will become a better friend, family member, and a more productive person. The worst feeling anyone can go through is experiencing depression. If you get invited to an event or a party and you don't want to go, there is no need to lie about how you feel. Your real friends will always understand, and if they are truly your friends they would want what is best for you. It is completely okay to first look after yourself.

For me, the research process for this book led to a transformative experience in my life. I interviewed close friends to gain a deeper understanding of their personal lives. They shared stories, details I had no idea about despite having known them for several years. It broke my heart to learn about my friends' experiences, yet perhaps I never had the foresight to ask them if they were okay. I was not anticipating them to completely open up. I, at times, forgot I was even writing a book. I found myself empathizing with them and almost hating myself for not asking these intimate questions sooner.

Throughout my time in college, I've learned the difference between understanding and not understanding yourself is by exercising humility. **Humility** is important because it encourages you to **seek feedback** and find creative ways to get better without hurting your progress or, better yet, without hurting yourself or the people around you.

RECOMMENDATION:
Take time, even if it's for only three minutes, to think about what you have to be grateful for. Times can be tough, especially right now with a global pandemic impacting everyone's lifestyles. But rather than dwelling on what we don't have, **try to focus on what we do have**.

PART III

HOW TO DATE YOURSELF

CHAPTER 8

EXPLORE THE WORLD AROUND YOU

MOTION CREATES EMOTION!
This section is about the importance of traveling. Given the circumstances of the current pandemic, travel restrictions have unfortunately brought our desires to explore other countries to a grinding halt. However, don't be discouraged because even if you are not able to travel outside the country or even outside your state, at least take time to explore your local surroundings.

Simply going for a walk in your neighborhood and reflecting on your life can do wonders for your mental state. It can also allow you to think of new ideas or to feel inspired by something you see. **Self-discovery is not a mission, but rather a journey you should take time to enjoy.**

The first method in searching for your best-self is to **travel**. Now this may be easier for others with the financial means to, let's say, travel to Europe, but you can truly learn a lot about yourself by simply placing yourself in a new environment. Literally taking the time to research a foreign country will give you a different perspective on how others live. You also might learn something new about yourself which you would not have learned if you stayed in your current environment. For example, you might realize going to art galleries or small intimate coffee shops by the Trocadero district in Paris brings an immense sense of joy.

Traveling can also have a profound impact on your mental health, as it provides a healthy alternative to exercising the body and the mind. Exploring will also teach you about different cultures, religions, and social norms.

I've learned a lot about myself through self-travel. Being able to explore the world alone gave me space to think about what I'm grateful for in my life, while also enjoying new surroundings and people. Once you feel comfortable traveling on your own, traveling with another person (your partner) makes the experience a whole lot more meaningful.

CNN made a list of the most romantic places to visit in 2020. Once the pandemic subsides, consider going with your partner to one of these places on their list of the **most romantic places to visit:**[23]

- *The Maldives*
- *Quebec City, Canada*
- *Tuscany, Italy*

---

23 Chris Dwyer, "The world's most romantic places," *CNN*, February 14, 2020.

- *Hawaii*
- *Charleston, South Carolina*
- *Botswana*
- *Paris, France*
- *Istanbul, Turkey*
- *Hoi An, Vietnam*
- *Bora Bora, French Polynesia*
- *Venice, Italy*
- *Buenos Aires, Argentina*
- *Kyoto, Japan*

Writer Irina Vishnevskaya from the *Huffington Post* wrote an article in 2017 titled "Your Honeymoon Is More Important Than Your Wedding —Here's Why."

I agree with her that weddings are a ton of fun to attend as a guest. The atmosphere is extremely positive and everyone is in a great mood. Weddings for the bride and groom, however, must be a massive headache. The institution of marriage is sacred and should be taken seriously, and so much goes into the process of planning that stress is guaranteed to come into play.

On the other hand, the honeymoon, even though it costs money, is a much more private adventure. Irina writes:[24]

> *"On your honeymoon, the two of you get to forget about the outside world and be you. Whatever that means to you—adventuring, hiking and camping, eating your way*

---

24 Irina Vishnevskaya, "Your Honeymoon Is More Important Than Your Wedding — Here's Why," *HuffPost*, October 23, 2017.

through your destination of choice or relaxing and being pampered. It's a chance for the two of you to reconnect after a whirlwind of a wedding planning process, and to re-solidify your relationship. You know, reign it back in, gather and collect yourselves and set the tone for the rest of your relationship together."

Unlike taking days off from work, your honeymoon might be one of the few times in your life where you are allowed to "splurge on travel" with societal rules on your side.

The honeymoon is a time where a couple does not need to stress about taking care of other people (family, friends, random guests). This may also be one of the last times when the couple will have the opportunity to enjoy complete privacy. Once a couple starts a family, it may become increasingly difficult to travel without their children.

There is also a sense of privacy when it comes to people trying to get details about how your honeymoon went. When you travel on your own or with your family, people will ask how it was. Perhaps there is pressure to post on social media all of your vacation spots and the different kinds of food you tried. The honeymoon is simply for the spouses to share a brief period of intimacy and escape the pressures of life while enjoying each other's company. Honeymoons are a chance for partners to become creative with ways to show their love. Typically, traveling to another location is a popular option for honeymooners because there is less chance a partner will become distracted or be reminded of their responsibilities back home or at work.

The most obvious, yet one of the most important reasons, to travel is you can not only learn about new cultures but also implement parts of that culture into your daily routine. When I was ten years old, my parents took me on a trip to Singapore and India (where my parents are from).

While visiting Singapore, we were introduced to feng shui. We absolutely fell in love with the concept of how cleanliness and organization impact the state of the body and mind. Feng shui translated means wind and water. Balancing mental and physical health is accomplished by balancing certain elements in your life such as earth, fire, metal, water, and wood.

Feng shui is not a form of religion nor does it encourage worshiping any spiritual elements. The purpose is to create harmony and balance within your home. For example, feng shui suggests not having any electronic devices in your bedroom (cell phone, laptop, television). Your bedroom is meant for rest, not to serve as an entertainment center. By removing electronics and clutter, you will have a sound sleep and will see your bedroom as a place to relax. Feng shui also encourages the use of positive imagery, surrounding yourself with pictures that make you feel happy, inspired, motivated, or calm.

The point of mentioning the practice of feng shui in this chapter is because my family and I would never have truly used this to our benefit had we not traveled outside the country. This is one of many examples of how you can learn more about yourself when you travel overseas.

To best understand yourself, you need to first take a look at your past and uncover both the pleasures and pain from it. Much like how we looked at the benefits of positive psychology, we want to take what we learned from our past experiences and use that to our advantage. This journey is completely up to you, the individual with a powerful soul. Try not to compare yourself with close friends or family, as searching for your best self is a completely unique experience. Let's take a look at some ways you can find your best self.

CHAPTER 9

EXERCISING POSITIVE HABITS

———

This goes hand in hand with the next chapter, which is about taking a break from social media. But in this chapter, we will be discussing self-discipline within the context of your everyday life, outside of any social media or technology. Much of one's depression can sometimes stem from a lack of organization both physically and mentally. Self-discipline is not as hard as it sounds. In fact, it feels good once you get the hang of it. The beauty of self-discipline is there is no such thing as perfection, but rather **progress**.

Much like learning to love your calendar, being self-disciplined in terms of your habits will change your life. I think the phrase "changing your life" should be rephrased to "chasing your dreams" because that is exactly what it is. Discipline can sometimes feel negative in that you have to live a strict life in order to attain results. Self-discipline doesn't mean that at all—it simply means doing what's best now versus what will cause pain in the long-term. It also means staying committed to something that will benefit you and the people around you.

According to psychologist Angela Duckworth from the University of Pennsylvania, *"Grit is about working on something you care about so much that you're willing to stay loyal to it."*[25] This mirrors the idea of being consistent on a particular activity or project over a long period of time. This requires an amalgam of passion, patience, enthusiasm, and endurance.

"Achievement is what happens when you take your acquired skills and use them."[25] Professor Duckworth also uses two equations in how to go from talent to achievement:[25]

- Talent **x** Effort = Skill
- Skill **x** Effort = Achievement

"Doing one thing better and better might be more satisfying than staying amateur at many different things."[25]

Self-discipline can be exercised regardless of age or where you are in life. It is never too late to form new habits that will improve your life. The strength of your character is guided by your decision making. Sometimes we may fall into temptation or say yes to activities, events, or even people, despite knowing that heading down that direction is not what's best for us.

---

25 Angela Duckworth, *"Grit"* (New York: Scribner, 2016), 44.

Harvard Business School Professor Steven R. Shallenberger, in his book *Becoming Your Best Self*, emphasizes the importance of being strong in your **moment of choice**. He writes: [26]

"When you don't live according to the principles and values that support your strength of character, you are usually thrown course and out of balance."

"Self-control is the ability to say no, in the face of temptation, and to take sustained action, despite the difficulty of a given challenge. At its heart, self-control requires the ability to delay gratification. More commonly, it's called discipline, or will. Without self-control, we can't accomplish almost anything of enduring value. And we rarely pay much attention to it."* [26]

We each have a moment of choice, so what goes through your mind during that moment? Do you think about the long-term consequences? Are you worried about the short-term consequences of not fitting in? Or are you simply trying to go

---

26   Steven R. Shallenberger, *"Becoming Your Best,"* (McGraw Hill Education, 2015), 5.

with the flow and enjoy whatever happens? We face temptations every day; temptation might be based on the individual, but nevertheless this is something we face and can hurt us, especially during times when we are most vulnerable. In that moment of temptation, the key is to quickly decide if that decision is worth compromising your long-term goals. An unfortunate reality of life is you can work hours, days, even years to accomplish a goal, yet it can take less than five seconds to lose it all. This is why your decision making is crucial to living a life of self-discipline.

Author Charles Duhigg, in his book *The Power of Habit*, discusses the three key behaviors of people when they develop a habit.[27]

1) **The Cue:** This serves as a trigger for your brain, making unconscious decisions that can lead to a particular habit.

2) **The Routine:** Acts or behavioral decisions (mental, emotional, physical) that lead up to the reward.

3) **The Reward:** When your brain figures out the benefits of the loop cycle and thus will remember it for the future which helps solidify the habit.

Our parents, from the time when we were young, tried their best to deter us from making bad decisions. Have you ever noticed it doesn't take much to tell a kid how to get in trouble, but it's much harder just to get them to behave properly?

---

27   Charles Duhigg, "*The Power of Habit*," (New York: Random House, 2014), 19.

This is why self-discipline is a skill that needs to be further developed, rather than unconsciously assuming our childhood took care of it all.

RECOMMENDATION:
Begin to ask yourself questions such as: "What am I interested in? What new skill would I like to learn? In what area of my life do I need to improve?" If you can find a small interest in addition to committing to learning more about that interest, then you might stumble upon a new passion within your life. Research shows people are happier in their careers when they feel like they have mastered their craft. Once you find your interest, investigate what kinds of options are available in the future for that particular interest. By doing so, you might have just started your path towards becoming an expert in your field of interest.

CHAPTER 10

PROTECT YOURSELF FROM SOCIAL MEDIA

———

I've used social media for a long time, even during the height of MySpace in 2005. Social media, overall, is a phenomenal logistical tool; you can get in touch with old friends, meet new ones, or even find a potential partner. From a personal standpoint, most of my past relationships were sparked either through Facebook Messenger or Instagram's direct message feature.

The social media channels we will primarily look at are Facebook, Instagram, Snapchat, and Twitter. The new kid on the block is TikTok, which has grown rapidly enough to create its own social media celebrities. Similar to Instagram, TikTok uses a discover page feature which is only comprised of videos rather than pictures.

Facebook and Twitter encourage dialogue, while Instagram and Snapchat are primarily image driven. Unlike the other social media channels, TikTok has transformed into a dance app thanks to the likes of the app's most popular user Charlie Demelio, who has over sixty million followers. Since people are staying inside due to the coronavirus pandemic, social media users have a lot more time on their hands and are more engaged than ever before.

The word "addicting" has been attached to the idea of social media since its invention. Social media comes at a large cost to your time and energy, which can be focused elsewhere. On average, users can spend between two to three hours on just one social channel. As far as opportunity cost is concerned, you could be spending those couple of hours more productively rather than scrolling through a news feed or liking posts that won't necessarily help you mature.

From my own experience, especially in college, I was much more productive with my time when I did not have social media to think about. This was because the stresses that come with social media (posting, liking other people's posts, editing, and updating) no longer played a role in my daily routine.

A feature which Instagram has been able to utilize well is the story feature, which allows users to post a video or picture for only twenty-four hours. Instagram users these days tend to look at stories more than liking an actual post. Posting stories can feel addicting, simply because it's a ton of fun and feels good to receive positive interaction for a brief period.

The main issue I've heard about social media is comparing yourself to others. I personally don't subscribe to that, but many do feel those posting "perfect parts of their lives" can make others feel inferior or even depressed. I don't think that's the intention of the person posting the photos, which is why I think it's better just to be happy for that person rather than resorting to feelings of jealousy. It sounds weird to say, but I feel it gives you freedom when you don't really care about how someone else's posts affect you. Yes, it can at times feel as if a user is posting material in an attempt to amplify their brand, but there are circumstances in which people can do the opposite and post only negative content and/or comments.

There are many benefits to social media that are at times underrated. For example, in writing this book I reached out to people I wanted to interview via Facebook. I'm not an avid user of Facebook. In fact, I have only posted a handful of times since the beginning of 2019. But I received a huge response and was able to interview almost every person who responded due to my outreach via Facebook. Social media can be a phenomenal way of gaining access to not only friends, but also celebrities.

For example, a simple direct message on Instagram or Twitter can be enough to get the attention of a major celebrity. In the past, gaining this kind of access meant either knowing someone close to that celebrity, or simply having the financial resources to meet them; this is not the case nowadays. Social media allows us to now communicate with anyone, and sometimes this can get people in trouble.

After giving my first TEDx Talk (which will be discussed further in the next chapter), we were invited to an end-of-session panel, which allowed all speakers to take questions from the audience. My topic was on depression: how to manage it through being grateful and helping others. One audience member sent in a question I thought was important pertaining to our mental health with social media. The question was, "how do we manage ourselves when we see others on social media posting about their best life?" I personally don't worry about what people post about themselves online. I've heard many times before that seeing others "show off" can feel intimidating and, at times, it can make someone (the viewer) feel inferior. I used to share that same sentiment; however, I now disagree.

To establish a healthy relationship with social media, it is important to note seeking external validation will not make you happy.

Receiving a certain amount of likes to validate your post is a superficial way to approach life. There are variables that go into play when determining the number of likes on a post. For example, the time of day in which you post counts, and what kind of audience follows you. Typically, early morning, evening, or the 8 to 9 p.m. timeframe sees the most user traffic, which will generate more likes. Even with that, not everyone will be viewing your post at the same time. People with a lot of followers may scroll through and miss your post, or they could simply be liking every post that they see.

*A finger tap on someone else's phone should not be a gateway to your happiness.

Like anything, I believe the key here is to have **self-control**. Social media can be used for a lot of good, whether it involves sharing a major accomplishment or raising money for a charity-—social media can help galvanize people. However, its usage should not consume most of your day. Think of social media more as a tool; these digital services can boost your platform or even your business, but don't use it recklessly.

On the contrary, there are also many positives to either not using or giving up engaging with social media completely. From my experience, I felt more relaxed and less stressed out when I did not use social media. I also found it much easier to focus on tasks and, in a way, I was able to act selfishly in terms of getting my responsibilities taken care of while also being able to help people less fortunate (raising money for the homeless).

RECOMMENDATIONS:

The reality is social media is almost becoming mandatory in terms of not only keeping in contact with your friends, but also advertising your own personal brand and staying updated on the current trends and events. As we dive deeper into a new digital world, staying updated has become extremely important for keeping in touch with modern culture and social movements. If you feel social media consumption is doing more harm than good, then take a step back and try to moderate your usage.

What has worked for me is utilizing a kind of "reward system." I set aside a specific time when I will be using social media for the day so I'm keeping track of time and making time my priority. I now only spend thirty minutes a day on all social media apps (e.g., Facebook, Instagram, Snapchat, TikTok, etc.). That is a drastic decline from my two-hour daily average. I believe that thirty to forty-five minutes per day is sufficient to stay updated with what's happening both locally and around the world, while also saving time to focus on more important activities that contribute to my happiness and success.

CHAPTER 11

HOW I MANAGED MY DEPRESSION

If you were to search images of depression on Google, you will see pictures of people physically isolated or showing signs of intense sadness. The reality of depression is it can easily be masked through smiles, laughter, and looking jovial in social situations.

A couple of months ago, I gave a TEDx Talk on how I managed my depression through being grateful, helping others, and reaching out. It was not easy to display my emotions in a public arena where it would be forever recorded and uploaded online. I've covered up my depression from friends and family for a long time and opened up about three years ago.

There is no remedy for overcoming depression, which is why the title of my TEDx Talk was "How I Managed My Depression." It's a constant oscillation between extreme feelings of happiness and deep sadness.

It's a realization this feeling may never go away, which I was completely okay with. The only reason why I'm including this chapter in the book is not so I can play the victim card, but rather to help that one person who may be feeling down and to let them know there is hope and lots of love.

I'm not a perfect human being by any means. The worst of my depression took place around 2013. I remember being in my apartment alone and thinking life had no meaning or purpose. I was heading in a decent direction in life but for some reason I felt more alone than ever.

I hung out with friends who had access to alcohol and other forms of drugs. My goal some days was to simply go out and party as hard as I could. If something happens then it just happens. Writing my suicide note felt like more of a relief than sad. As I was writing it, I felt my problems evaporate. I saw the real value in everything around me such as my family, career, school, and relationships, but all of that diluted and for a moment became an irrelevant part of my life.

There were many times I failed to actually go through with it. One time I was adamant that day was the day. To add some humor, I ended up getting so trashed I forgot to go through with it. In the end, I realized ending my life was not worth it simply because I began to see it as a form of quitting. "If I feel mistreated or not worthy, why should I be the one hurting myself?" The first step for me was to accept responsibility for my actions and take full ownership of myself moving forward.

I'll tell you this: I wouldn't be writing this book right now had I gone through with those negative thoughts. If you are currently in an impossible bind, trust that there is always a way out! The road to recovery is a journey with no shortcuts. Being focused on the destination will only drive you insane. Focusing and practicing small, good habits will truly transform your life in the long run.

While I understand the brain may have some deficiencies (for example, lack of serotonin), I personally did not take any medication nor have I ever gone to therapy. I've had many friends who have also experienced depression, which would unfortunately escalate because of the drugs they were taking. Therapy has proven to be helpful to my friends who have experienced depression. If you feel the need to talk to someone, I highly suggest doing so.

The first time I opened about my depression was with a friend of mine in Richmond. I sent him a text saying I wanted to talk because I was feeling down. The fact that he listened and took the time to come over to my apartment just to hear me out truly meant the world to me (if you are reading this, I sincerely thank you and will never forget it).

The most frightening aspect of experiencing depression is that as soon as he left my apartment, I knew I would have to face myself all alone. Looking back, life was looking pretty good at the time, but it didn't feel like it.

While I was going through most episodes of my depression back in 2013, I remember expressing it to people and they had no idea what it meant; they sort of saw it as being "overly sad." Now that times have changed, I've noticed an alarming amount of people mentioning they have anxiety *and* depression before I even get to know their name.

Another critical reason why I'm choosing to talk about depression in this book is because I want to make sure this statement is emphasized throughout: **you are not responsible for someone else's happiness**. While self-happiness is important for any relationship, so is the happiness of the individual you are in a relationship with.

There's a quote from Will Smith that I love, which highlights the importance of happiness within his own marriage: [28]

"You can make a person smile, you can make a person feel good, you can make a person laugh, but whether or not a person is happy deeply, totally, and utterly is out of your control.

Her happiness was her responsibility and my happiness was my responsibility and we decided we were going to find our individual internal, private joy and then we were going to present ourselves to the relationship and to each other, already happy.

Not coming to each other, begging with our empty cups out demanding she fill my cups and demanding she meet my needs. It's unfair and it's kind of unrealistic and can be destructive to place the responsibility for your happiness on anybody other than yourself."

---

28 Tita Cara, "Will Smith Explains Why It's Not His Responsibility To Make His Wife Happy," *Haute Living*, February 21, 2018.

From personal experience, no matter what you do there is no way you can make someone else happy if they are not happy with themselves.

My dear friend Michael James has been nothing but a quality person in my life. He is the type of guy who will send you a text saying, "*Have a Dope Day.*" It may be something as small as that, but it still means the world to me. He's truly one of those good guys who are hard to come by. He grew up in a loving family and was overall a good kid. During high school he loved playing sports, but experienced concussions from football and lacrosse. After high school, life became blurry and he began to feel like it was almost "*not worth living.*" The temptations of life can kind of take hold, which led to his state of depression. In the midst of his depression, he moved to Los Angeles, wanting to take his own life. It was chaos he could control, but the search for stability was at his core. Those dark times made him into who he is today. From that gray period, he is beginning to get some color back into his life. What brings him happiness is seeing other people succeed. This is a rare quality to find in people these days, but this is my favorite quality in anybody, especially in Michael.

I currently manage my depression by listening to strong leaders who have experienced difficult challenges in their lives and excelled despite the odds. Author, speaker, and Navy SEAL David Goggins really spoke to some of my insecurities when I read his book *Can't Hurt Me*. He discusses developing a callous in your mind and states **we are the heroes in our own stories**.

If you're not familiar with his story, here's a quick rundown: Goggins faced a ton of trauma in his childhood and was extremely overweight. The odds of him making it to any kind of special forces, let alone the elite American navy seals seemed almost impossible.

Navy seal training is the toughest military training on the planet. During the BUD's (Basic Underwater Demolition) phase of SEAL training, the recruits must go through hell week, which is an entire week of running miles with only three to four hours total of sleep. Goggins made it through the toughest training in the world by callusing his mind. He didn't listen to the negative voices in his head saying, "stop or quit!" He says that *"the cost of quitting would be lifelong purgatory."*[29]

His book was so intense I felt like I would be a quitter if I put it down. I was truly motivated by his words and I hope his voice can do the same for you. Here are some of my favorite quotes from his book:[29]

- *"Choose any competitive situation you're in right now. Who is your opponent? Is it your teacher, coach, your boss, an unruly client? No matter how they're treating you there is one way to not only earn their respect but turn the tables. Excellence."*
- *"Know the terrain, know yourself, and you'd better know your adversary in detail. Know why you're in the fight and stay in the fight!"*

---

29   David Goggins, *"Can't Hurt Me,"* (Lioncrest Publishing, 2018), 122.

- *"Your goal is to make them watch you achieve what they could never have done themselves."*

RECOMMENDATION:

If you are going through depression, it is important to surround yourself with people who believe in and support you. During the hardest days of depression, watching speeches on YouTube, especially by Martin Luther King, which helped inspire me when I felt the loneliest. One of my favorite Dr. King's speeches is *"**What is your life's Blueprint?**"*

PART IV

HOW TO DATE OTHERS

CHAPTER 12

A DIFFERENT WAY OF DATING

———

In this chapter, I would like to highlight how couples date differently from the traditional norms we are used to seeing. I have interviewed a lot of demographics for this book. Yet, it was my own parents who bring an extremely diverse perspective on marriage and dating.

My dad is South Indian and my mother is Anglo-Indian. For quick context, during the British rule in India, European soldiers would have relationships with, and many would marry, local Indian women. This led to the birth of the Anglo-Indian community, which is a cultural combination of both European and Indian descent. My parents met and dated while in India when my mom was in her senior year of college her late teens. My dad was in his early twenties and already had a bachelor of commerce, but did not actively pursue a career at the time as he had planned to visit his sister and her family in Australia and then the US. As a result, he was in between jobs when he met my mom. Their first date was simply getting to know each other. There was no fancy dinner planned; instead, they decided to go watch a movie and take a walk on the beach. My dad was pleasantly surprised when my mom offered to share the cost of the movie tickets. Being a student and an only child, she had a little more pocket money than he did. Moreover, my mom did not believe in a man paying on the first date, especially if he didn't have a job. On several of their future dates, it was only natural for them to share expenses. The point is that, within their relationship, they didn't follow the traditional rules of dating where "the man has to pay for everything."

It wasn't long before they both secured jobs in multi-national companies and decided to get married. Since both came from different backgrounds due to their heritage, their respective families had different ideas about their wedding plans. It can be quite controversial dating someone from a different background even if they are from the same country. Indians typically (in those days) did not date other castes and were traditional when it came to marriage. My parents simply refused to listen to others and instead focused on their own happiness as a couple.

Rather than the bride's family paying for the entire wedding as was the custom, my parents shared their wedding expenses. They saved enough money to have their reception at a five-star hotel in the city of Madras, now Chennai.

Fast forward thirty-five years later, both are successful in their respective careers. Since my mother paid for those movie tickets years ago (a good investment, she claims), my father now buys her whatever she wants. As a couple, they firmly believe in saving most of their money and not over-spending on non-essentials. The key concept in a partnership, marriage, or dating should require both parties to not only effectively communicate but to manage their finances and other needs as a team. For them, I noticed communicating and sharing the same religious faith were key ingredients for their successful marriage. Communication and faith allow them to solve problems and establish a common vision for the benefit of the family. I'm also a practicing Catholic simply because my parents share the same faith and I've seen it work for them.

How has this idea changed over time? Millennials, whom I've spoken to, believe in separating their finances and having "their own individual spending money." Partners don't feel like it's their duty to report what they wish to spend money on. The problem with this philosophy is that there is already miscommunication, which could lead to possible mistrust down the road.

I interviewed a college friend of mine, Faye Al-Saadoon (we'll discuss more about her experiences in the dating world, as a young Muslim woman). She gave an interesting perspective in that most of her dates were with men who practiced a different religion than her. She explains that:

"In the short term, it can be easier to date someone of a different faith because you are going into this blind without any form of expectation, versus facing important questions immediately such as how religious are they, what parts of the faith do they bring into and leave out of the dating scene?

*"In the long run, however, partners of different faiths would face more questions about marriage. What faith would the children practice? How would each other's families react? Will my actions reflect negatively on my family? How will this picture that's posted reflect on my family? It can get complicated just thinking about it. **But as a couple we can inspire each other.**"*

Values, such as honesty, are important, and being clear with your partner, whether positive or negative, is equally important. Trust, loyalty, and ambition are also important values which shouldn't be second guessed. Be true to yourself—you know who you are and you know what's right. Be clear and honest about your intentions; forget about putting up a shield that disguises who you truly are.

Faye describes surrounding yourself with the people you love as "pure happiness." Family is a top priority in her life; decisions are made based on what is best for her family and finding ways to support them later. It makes their lives easier. You are the representative of your family, no matter where you are and where you go. Your **actions**, your **words**, and your **behavior** will always be connected back to them.

Growing up in one of the richest counties in America, twenty-six-year-old Heather Wald was frequently pressured by her peers into finding a man with a high-paying and respected professional career. Especially during high school, this message was frequently echoed into the hallways of her conscience. She was afraid of the social consequences if she were to pursue a female companion, especially in a predominately white and ultra-conservative community.

I was her best friend throughout those high school years and even I was shocked when she told me she's in a relationship with not one, but *two* women. Dating women was a completely new and massive transition for her. She explained, "*being attracted to other girls felt like losing your virginity all over again.*" She went on to say she felt more emotionally and sexually open with girls and views guys primarily as friends. But still, because of her upbringing, she said she was "*still watching other people and what I was supposed to be instead of watching out for myself.*"

Heather is no longer self-conscious about her attraction to women and has embraced her new sense of self. She is currently involved in a polyamorous relationship, which is a romantic relationship involving three or more parties. It took much of her early adult life to find out who she was and what she was into.

She was still living in an environment where there was not a strong support system for the LGBTQ community. It is only when she stepped out of bounds and traveled to other places that she began to feel more comfortable with her identity: "*I'm not a normal person, I'm going to be outside the norm. I had to get away from everyone else that was normal in order to find it. When I started stepping into the LGBTQ community, they were simply so accepting of who I am and were not judgmental.*"

"*When it came to dating guys, it was only after around the six-month mark where I felt that this wasn't the right fit for me.*" With a guy, there was always this pressure to dress up, look nice, and maintain his interest so he does not leave for another girl. Dating a girl felt like the opposite in that there was no pressure to, for example, put on makeup because she didn't feel she needed to compete with other straight girls. *"I can have a bad day or feel sad, and she'll still find me attractive. If she has an emotional day, there was an immediate understanding and there was no judgement."*

Within the polyamorous social circles, Heather explained that *"even though Emily is my girlfriend, if I went on a date with someone else she would be fine. We have each other's emotional support, and if I need a different sexual support I have the flexibility to go find that."* Another interesting aspect of polyamorous relationships is the idea of re-engineering family structure, as Heather points out when she says, *"the idea of having kids with three moms really makes me happy."*

In terms of jealousy, much like any other relationship, there needs to be an open line of communication, especially when recognizing other attractive people. In a three-way relationship, communication needs to be completely open—otherwise a brief disconnect could lead to major miscommunication or a potential avoidable breakup.

Heather's advice for men and women seeking a committed long-term relationship:

"Be patient, put yourself in your partner's shoes, and just try to understand by saying 'I hear you.'"

Dating shouldn't be about following rules, but about having respect for the person you're with. Communication is the key to any relationship; this is not a one-size-fits-all kind of deal. It's okay to be different, as long as you and your partner are being true to yourselves.

CHAPTER 13

HOW TO AVOID RED FLAGS

———

The consequences of moving into a relationship too quickly can result in one or both parties involved overlooking each other's Red Flags. A Red Flag refers to a toxic, deceitful, abusive, or dangerous attribute a person may exhibit.

Red flags, in any kind of relationship, can harm us emotionally and sometimes physically. It can, at times, be extremely difficult to identify certain attributes in the beginning of a relationship, especially if the individual is crafty at hiding these kinds of warning signs. **Red Flags are unique to everyone but can be equally as dangerous and must not be ignored.**

First, we need to look at some reasons behind why we might ignore warning signs. Then, we will look at how to identify these signs of danger at the start of any relationship. Reflect and write down some of the red flags you've either noticed in past relationships or need to watch out for before beginning a new relationship.

Generally, once you find someone who meets some of the criteria on the potentially long list of standards you have for a new partner, you might tend to overlook some warning signs in an attempt to accelerate the relationship for fear of losing your new love interest. This is where the momentum of the relationship can change quickly. The danger is when you begin to forgive some of the bad behavior or unhealthy habits of your partner. Whether intentional or unintentional, accepting bad behavior can (depending on your criteria or standards you have set), in a weird way, also decrease the level of interest of the person you are trying to attract. Think of it this way—they may think "wow, if this person is letting me treat them this way, then there's no way I could be in a relationship with them," which brings us to the importance of loving yourself first!

An example of a major Red Flag is when a person violates your personal space. Whether it involves a male or female, consent is extremely important to talk about, especially since it is the most important form of "physical" communication in any relationship. A dear friend of mine, Emma Earnest, lived in Los Angeles where she worked as a professional model and actress. During her time on the west coast, Emma was exposed to a whole new dating culture within the realm of the television industry. She loves to explore her sensual side while at the same time ensuring she is treated with respect.

While working on a project, Emma mentioned she was violated by a guy she once viewed as a close male friend (out of respect for her, I will not provide all of the details of what happened). Not only did he betray her trust, but he completely crossed the line, leaving her with a lot of internal pain that can't be entirely healed. This is not the first nor the last time this has happened to her. Because of her line of work, some men in the industry like to use her modeling career as an opportunity to take advantage of her vulnerability and fulfill their own perverted agendas.

She is completely aware of this climate and has complete control over what kind of people she wants to surround herself with. Emma is one of the strongest people I know and does not allow her expressiveness to define who she is; she is a grown woman with boundaries—yet grown men try to still ignore them to this day. She says, "*just because I may dress a certain way does not give people permission to violate my personal space. Unfortunately, it still happens all the time, especially in crowded places.*"

Emma, who is currently pursuing a degree in social work, brought up the concept of "intimacy theory," otherwise known as "the triangular theory of love."[30] This theory, which was orchestrated by psychologist Robert Sternberg, articulates three kinds of love on three different scales:

a. **Intimacy:** Describes feelings of connection, closeness, and warmth between two or more people.
b. **Passion:** A drive or motivation that leads to feelings of physical arousal, attraction, and heightened levels of intense romantic experiences.

---

30   Robert J. Sternberg, "Duplex Theory of Love: Triangular Theory of Love and Theory of Love as a Story," *Robertjsternberg,* accessed 2020.

c. **Commitment:** A conscious decision to maintain feelings of love.

The purpose of this theory is to show how these three components interact with each other. The diagram of this theory, which is shaped like an equilateral triangle, represents balance within a relationship. How does this theory relate to Red Flags? Think of it this way—not every relationship will feature a person who has substantial flaws or personality traits that exhibit bad behavior. Sometimes couples break up due to a deficiency in other areas of the relationship. It is okay to break up with someone if they don't meet your desired criteria. While no one is perfect and it's important to love people for who they are, you still have every right to be with someone who ignites feelings of passion and intimacy or encourages you to want to desire commitment.

It is extremely important to be completely honest with yourself about what you want and to communicate your desires to your partner as soon as possible. The longer you are in a relationship with that person, the more serious the relationship becomes (obviously). By being honest in the beginning, you will be able to enjoy each other's company rather than worrying about uncovering potentially toxic habits. Again, it's not easy to accomplish all of this in the beginning, but try your best to save yourself heartache in the future.

My close friend David, whom I mentioned earlier in the book, has been in a lot of serious relationships. Marriage was discussed at one point with some of his former partners. When I asked him about Red Flags, he responded:

*"Red Flags are rough because most times they're in plain sight, yet we still seek ways to deny them. **A Red Flag comes in many shapes and forms**. The ones I've come into contact with the most are people who are pathological liars, people who degrade you because of their own insecurities, people who avoid communication, and people who would rather hold grudges and stay in a constant state of hate instead of resolving the issues at hand. The best way to tear down Red Flags, in my opinion, is to not tolerate them. To have respect for yourself and make it clear what you're looking for in a healthy and mature relationship."*

Hailey Lamb is a fun-loving country girl from Salmon, Idaho. I met her while partying with our mutual friend David. I asked Hailey about her opinion on the topic of Red Flags in dating. She replied:

*"In some of the relationships I've been in, I've had to deal with a lot of "**love bombing**," which is when guys come off overly strong by saying comments like 'I really need you, or I've never felt this way about a person before.' It can feel good in the short term, but after a while it begins to feel overbearing and somewhat claustrophobic.*

Another example is if you and I are unofficially dating, you can obviously do whatever you want. But when you begin lying about the things you're doing when we're not together, it shows either you don't respect me as a person or you're just completely arrogant. Either way, I'm not going to put myself through that. I'm here to help better you but I'm not going to compromise my values or morals to make you happy. That is your responsibility.

*On the flip side, I do appreciate men who are honest, intelligent, hardworking, and are happy with themselves. **The ability to communicate effectively is extremely important to me**. If I can have an intelligent conversation with them, it's the biggest turn on. Because, don't get me wrong, I've dated some men in the past who halfway through a sentence would stop me and say they don't understand."*

Hailey is right in that we are not responsible for the happiness of someone else (this will be stressed a couple more times in the book). She also brings up a valid point when it comes to listening. It doesn't matter which sex is involved—the ability to patiently listen is one of the most important components of maintaining a healthy relationship. Any kind of relationship involves a lot of give and take and should never be a one-way street. If the person you're currently with does not listen to you, then end the relationship immediately. Life is too short to spend your valuable time around people who don't hear your thoughts, feelings, and aspirations.

An interesting trend I've learned from interviewing men and women is that there seems to be a battle between internal and external desires. The majority of men whom I've interviewed, when discussing relationships, voiced mainly the displeasures within themselves. The reasons why relationships in the past have not worked out sometimes had little or nothing to do with the person they were in a relationship with. The problem, according to them, was the lack of progress they were making in their own lives.

There is a lot of pressure on men, especially when it comes to relationships. Traditional male stereotypes may pressure them into thinking they should provide complete financial support, hold in their emotions of vulnerability and pain to show toughness, and always get along with their partner's friends. Some guys interviewed have stated that when they are too vulnerable to their partner during an argument, it may result in their partner using their vulnerabilities against them (it can work the other way too). This may be a reason why guys, as they get older, tend to be less vulnerable and more sheltered. Men are incredibly emotional, yet they are told it is not masculine to act as such.

With women, the trend has been that many of their relationships ended due to issues with their former partners. Now this is tricky because in no way should we eliminate the fact that women go through internal pressures, too. While they explained their relationships, a common difference between them and their former partner was a difference in vision. Relationships would often end due to a difference in long-terms goals, specifically involving travel. Patterns in some of these interviews indicated men preferred more routine in their environment and expressed less of a desire to travel or go out. Women saw this as a Red Flag, in the sense of feeling fenced in by a relationship. This may not always be the case; sometimes the opposite can occur. But what's important is both partners communicate their tastes or preferences in lifestyle early in their relationship so as to avoid a disconnect later on.

In terms of patterns, it seems as though women felt "**relationship claustrophobia**," in which the relationship was preventing them from achieving goals they would be likely to achieve if they were single. Many women expressed that the search for the perfect man was not their main priority. In fact, older women tend to become more understanding of men. However, this does not mean that they will tolerate BS. Older women will be more upfront with what they want which is a major plus for men, who should not take that for granted.

The displeasure men find within themselves also comes from the lack of progress they might be making in their lives and ironically, they are the ones who are more worried about finding a mate than women. The reality for most men is they simply need financial security and to be making progress in their careers to have some level of comfort in their lives.

The way to fix this can be done in two ways: empathize more and physically move out of your comfort zone—this goes for both men and women. In terms of internal communication, arguing should not involve intense yelling and screaming, especially when both parties eventually reach parenthood. Screaming and yelling only does damage to your children and those memories can never be erased. Arguments should instead become more of a discussion.

Even though it is extremely tough to not become emotional during an argument (saying all of this is much easier said than done), both sexes should allow just the power of their words and not the volume of their voices to do the talking. Irrational and loud yelling matches can sometimes result in domestic or even physical abuse. This should never be an outcome and unfortunately everyone, no matter how good, can become susceptible to being on the other end of this situation.

Last but not least, we definitely have to discuss the topic of jealousy. *"Threats are cruel manipulations by those who would control us. Warnings are signals to alert us to dangers that could harm us."*[31] My friend Casey Jones was in a relationship with another friend of mine, Jake Salewski. Even though they are no longer together, they had a healthy form of communication. While working on her bachelor's degree, Casey worked as a part-time waitress and she relayed some of her experiences of getting hit on while on the job.

While working, she would often get hit on by patrons of the restaurant who would give her their phone number on the receipt (how classy!). It was not a problem for Jake, but even he admits it was a lot to handle sometimes. Jake is overall not a jealous person and was extremely supportive of Casey in whatever she wanted to pursue in life. Casey says, *"if either one of us had an issue, we would discuss it over wine later that night. We also took time for ourselves, so we were not constantly in each other's faces."* They both encouraged each other to find alone time because they would come back together stronger and more fulfilled.

Author of the book *Unveiled* and a friend mine from the previous chapter, Faye, was also kind enough to share what kind of Red Flags she might see in someone. She said:

"When going out to dinner with someone, I try to notice how they treat the waiter or waitress. For me, it is a mirror into a person's upbringing, manners, and their morals based off how

---

31   Robert H. Schuller, *"Hours of Power,"* (New York: HarperSanFrancisco, 2004), 143.

they treat someone that is, by societal standards, beneath them. It is definitely something I take note of.

A Red Flag I notice is when a person makes racially insensitive comments or labels from the very beginning (typically involving jokes about being Arab or Muslim). These comments are uncomfortable because it exoticizes my nationality. It can backfire when someone is trying to be appear as 'woke' but instead it comes across as racist."

Another important Red Flag Faye mentioned is when a person constantly measures or tallies the amount of money spent in the relationship. For example, *"I've done this much for you and you've only done this certain amount."*

 *Keeping count of actions and deeds is not healthy in any form of relationship.

Most of us will have at least one, if not a few, significant relationships during our lifetime. Our first intimate encounters may be more challenging because we're new to the experience of forming an intimate bond with another person and may not really know what we're doing or what to expect. But time and experience should help us navigate through future relationships in a much better way.

It is essential to get to know *yourself* in every possible way before you move into a committed relationship. Often, individuals go in search of a relationship without this essential knowledge. But how can you ever hope to know another individual if you don't know yourself first? How can you address another's needs and desires if you're disconnected from your own? As obvious as these issues may appear and as much as you may feel you understand them, it should come as no surprise that what initially seems unimportant may take on greater significance as insights occur over the course of the relationship. In retrospect, individuals are often baffled about their own behavior and expectations in a relationship.

Abigail Brenner, MD, from *Psychology Today* wrote a fantastic piece on how to uncover Red Flags in the beginning stages of a relationship. Her article starts off by posing self-reflection questions about what initially attracted you to your current or past partner:[32]

1. *What attracted you to this person initially?*
2. *Did the attraction last?*
3. *Was your fantasy about this person—what you imagined or assumed to be true—validated in reality?*
4. *How long did the relationship last? Did revelations during the course of the relationship change your mind?*
5. *What was the deal breaker?*
6. *Do any patterns, similarities from relationship to other relationships, emerge?*

Brenner writes that it is vital to ask these questions in the beginning, before solid opinions are made. I've looked at a lot of lists involving Red Flags, but I believe these are the

---

32 Abigail Brenner, "10 Relationship Red Flags," *Psychology Today*, July 29, 2014.

most important Red Flags to look out for simply because it involves your own mental and physical well-being.

HERE ARE SIXTEEN EXAMPLES OF RED FLAGS YOU SHOULD WATCH OUT FOR IN ANY KIND OF RELATIONSHIP (ROMANTIC/SOCIAL/PROFESSIONAL):

1. **Inability to Communicate**: As we've already discussed frequently throughout this book, communication is vital for any relationship to succeed. Lacking communication, no matter the stage in the relationship, will only lead to more arguments and sometimes can lead to cheating. Communication is a sign of partnership; honesty is also another important element. You can communicate all you want, but if it's not honest communication both parties will be wasting each other's time.

2. **Lack of Maturity**: Similar to the importance of communication, maturity is crucial to maintaining a healthy relationship. Especially if the relationship is becoming more serious, you have to think about your partner as a parent and a spouse. These roles are serious and take a ton of time and commitment. Being with someone who lacks maturity will not only be frustrating but could also put you in some compromising situations. Traits of a mature person should include *"taking care of themselves, managing their finances and personal space, holding onto a job, and making plans for their life and future."*32

3. **Uncontrollable and Erratic Behavior**: A relationship is a partnership, and each person's behavior is a reflection of their partner. Acting erratic is not a good look for the

person involved or the relationship as a whole. This isn't high school—life has consequences that can permanently destroy a person's reputation. Do not make the mistake of allowing someone to enter your life who might do more harm than good.

4. **Toxic Circles**: Who do they surround themselves with? A person is a reflection of their friends. If the person you're with seems normal but his inner circle is not, take note because it's only a matter of time before your partner begins to exhibit some of those characteristics.

5. **Excessive Jealousy**: Do they constantly want to check your phone? Are they keeping tabs on everything you do? The sign of a healthy relationship is when individuality is allowed. Alexis, from earlier in the book, said marriage is *"two lives merging into one."* The person you're with should respect that you also have a life. As long as you are being honest and faithful, there should be no need for a helicopter partner. Trust goes a long way.

6. **Relationship Insecurity**: Constantly paying attention to personal insecurities will only further hurt the relationship. Yes, it is okay to have insecurities like everyone else, but don't let those thoughts take over your life. It is not worth it. The negative effects insecurities can have on a relationship may result in your partner becoming less attracted to you because it represents your self-doubt. You can't be a leader of a family if you keep doubting yourself.

7. **An Unforgiving Past**: *"Behaviors that are suspect, illegal activities, and addictive behaviors that haven't been*

resolved and continue into your relationship are obvious red flags."32 It's important to understand people can change for the better, but they can also change for the worse. A past can sometimes be a great indication of maturity and humility, but if they are still exhibiting similar traits from their past then it's time to move on.

8. **Not Faithful or Honest**: There is no excuse for someone to cheat on you!. If they feel differently about the relationship, it is their job to communicate how they feel. If they are unable to do that, then they are not worth your time. Cheating can have serious ramifications on a person's mental state as it's seen as a sign of betrayal.

    4. Don't be that person. 2. Always communicate your feelings if you are attracted to someone else. 3. If you suspect your partner is being shady or outright cheating, then get them out of your life! You don't deserve that kind of treatment.

9. **Refusing to Meet Needs of the Relationship**: You can't fix everybody. If they are not willing to put in the work, there is no way the relationship can succeed in the long term. Always communicate your needs from the beginning and make sure your partner does the same. This is a two-way street and the only way it is going to work is if both of you are on the same track.

10. **Physically or Emotionally Abusive**: Physical and emotional abusers need to be removed from your life immediately! It may be harder to detect someone who is emotionally abusive but remember: words can hurt just as much as physical pain. If you feel like the person you're

dating is being disrespectful toward you, it is best you leave now and take back ownership of your life. No one has the right to disrespect you, no matter who they are.

11. **Rude to People in the Service Industry:** Similar to what Faye mentioned earlier in the chapter, how they treat a person who serves them (waiters or waitresses) is a direct reflection of their character.

12. **Differences of Opinion Regarding Finances:** This depends on the age of the couple involved, but the older you get the more important financial stability becomes. When the topic of starting a family arises, financial management is extremely vital for the health of the family especially in the long term.

13. **Do They Care about Your Mental Health?** Are they supportive of your mental health? This is a must. Relationships can worsen the damage if not taken care of. Toxic people will further accelerate feelings of depression which can lead to sometimes life-threatening consequences.

14. **What Do They Say about You When You Are Not Around?** If a person talks behind someone's back frequently to you, then get rid of that person. You never know what they could be saying behind your back.

15. **Are They Taking Time to Focus on Themselves?** This may be a flag you don't hear a lot of. But it is important to ask yourself if the person you are with is taking time to enhance themselves. If they are too focused on the

relationship, that could be an indicator the relationship is not as healthy as it appears.

16. **Always Blames Their Exes**: Pay attention to how they described the person they used to date. (This can also be applied to interviewing potential candidates in the workforce regarding former employers). You want to see how they interpret their past. If they come across as angry and claim their exes "were all crazy," there is a high possibility the relationship they are seeking will not work out. They also might talk about you in a similar negative tone behind your back.

To put it more bluntly, both parties in the relationship should stop using their weaknesses against each other. Otherwise it will result in strong distrust between the two, thus negatively affecting the relationship in the long term (referring to a breakup). It is also important to not only ask yourself what are some of the Red Flags you see in a person, but to ask the more difficult question of what are some of your own Red Flags? Nobody is perfect, but having a strong level of self-awareness will not only help you in dating, but also in your professional life.

WHAT RED FLAGS DO YOU NEED TO WATCH OUT FOR?
1) Describe personality traits.

_____

_____

_____

2) What does history say about them?

_____

_____

_____

3) How do they treat others?

_____

_____

_____

4) How would you describe their level of maturity? How important is that to you?

_____

_____

_____

5) Describe their passions or goals. Does it align with what you want?

_____

_____

_____

CHAPTER 14

CULTIVATING HEALTHY RELATIONSHIPS

———

Entering arelationship is no easy task. It's not easy to let another person into your life, introduce them to your family, or allow them to access your vulnerability. No individual is perfect, nor is any relationship. A healthy relationship does not just magically appear; it takes a lot of communication, understanding, and empathetic actions with your partner. Sometimes couples don't even have a lot in common, but what makes them work well is that they both enjoy each other's company and are transparent about their needs and wants.

I feel it is important to understand relationships through the experience of others. Here I have specifically chosen people I know, simply because I have witnessed their relationships develop through the years, as well as watched them grow as individuals. Interestingly enough, some of the couples I will mention in this chapter have split up but still have mutual respect for each other.

After interviewing these couples, I found communication about long-term goals was the most important characteristic pertaining to those who were the happiest. This might sound fake because how can you tell whether or not a couple is happy? Throughout these interviews, I looked at the amount of time (total duration they spent with each other), the seriousness of the relationship, and interviewed them individually on how they felt the relationship is going.

The term "communication" can often mean something broad, so let's condense it a little more. Communication in a relationship is not just about sharing your most vulnerable thoughts, but also your emotional needs and wants which is strengthened by **trust-building actions**. Trust is broken when there is a breakdown in communication; in a much larger picture, cheating does not happen overnight (although it technically could). Couples who experienced cheating in the past said it occurred when one partner felt distant from the other.

Having experienced being cheated on, there are many variables that may result in this happening. It can happen spontaneously, be calculated, or both. When it happens, it feels like the ultimate betrayal. It's imperative to recognize it may not be a reflection of who you are, but more so who they are. Therefore, being honest with what you want in the beginning is crucial to understanding what's best for the relationship. Sometimes the truth may not be what you want, but it may save you from a ton of heartache in the future.

As a young, humble, and independent woman, Casey Jones has found her life's calling. Influenced by her father, Casey currently works as a call center specialist at the National Center for Missing and Exploited Children. Throughout her early childhood, she was not exposed to healthy familial or social relationships. However, her father was a guardian angel who helped shape her into the woman she is today.

Her father was adamant Casey and her younger brother Billy experience the struggles of life together and not go through it alone. Having witnessed it firsthand, their bond is truly special and makes a person like myself contemplate the real meaning behind taking care of family. Through being responsible at an early age for having her brother's back, Casey realized the importance of keeping the right people in your life as well as focusing on your own happiness.

A critical concept that Casey brushed upon during our interview is who you surround yourself with is equally as important. She says:

> *"I'm a big believer that every single choice you make, something else will result from it. Life is about the choices you make; sometimes one small decision is the difference between life and death. For example, think about one person who got a cut on their finger on their way to the World Trade Center on 9/11 and stopped at the CVS, so they're not dead. If everything happens for a reason, then you should do the things you want to. That's also why my mindset now is very much doing what makes me happy. I'm never the kind of person that is going to agree to do something I don't want to do."*

This mindset of doing what you want to do has trickled into her relationships with people. Casey does not use proximity as a reason for hanging around a certain group, but rather she values her time as well as valuing the time of others.

As I've mentioned in the beginning chapters, there is always a cost with the actions you take and the time you spend on an idea, activity, or person(s). This approach has made her into an outstanding friend.

This may sound biased, but I owe the success of my TEDx Talk to her support and encouragement on the day of the event. She was the only person constantly giving me assurance the event will work out, and it came at the best possible time. This is why having a circle of people you trust is the key to maintaining long-lasting and healthy relationships. People come and go, but the ones who truly love you will support your mission, in addition to making sacrifices to ensure you succeed.

She describes her favorite memory of her father during her junior year in high school where she says, "*after prom, all of my girlfriends came back to my house for a sleepover and we all walked in drunk at 2 a.m. and my dad had a whole spread of breakfast, water, and Advil ready for us. He was the coolest dad ever.*"

Being in a relationship is more about the journey and not the destination. Thinking about the future too much can be detrimental to enjoying the moment that's right in front of you. Thinking too much about the future may result in your partner or even you being absent from the journey. One of the worst feelings in the world is feeling alone when you are in a relationship with someone.

As we've recognized in the beginning of this book, **the biggest investment you will make in your life is the person you choose to spend the rest of your life with**. It is important to establish trust in the beginning by being honest with yourself. Moving into a relationship just to feel comfortable is not fair to the other person. If you want something casual, take ownership of that and look for something casual. We communicate with the world by communicating with ourselves.

We also have to recognize people, including us, will change either for the better or worse. We must monitor this change to recognize whether this is either helping or hindering our progress.

A professional model and an avid Baltimore Orioles fan from Falls Church, Virginia, Mary was generous enough to reflect on her family life and her lessons from past relationships. She grew up monetarily poor and, at times, relied on food stamps to get by. She mentioned her family would apply for a program called "Christmas in July," where people would come to her house and provide construction work for free. Her mom also saved money by locating good deals and not overspending on essentials like boxes of food (which were at times expired), diapers, and other home maintenance supplies. Because of her mom's knack to not overspend, Mary qualified to receive a free education at her high school because she fell within the poverty bracket.

Right after high school, making ends meet was a major concern, so she entered the workforce instead of taking the traditional college route. College is incredibly expensive and would have added a considerable amount of debt.

Diving into Mary's personal life is important because it strongly impacts the kinds of guys and people she may be exposed to. She explains that *"having your head on your shoulders is vital to not allowing yourself to f**k up. Once you get past a certain level, you might get sucked into that life. When you are poor, you might get surrounded by certain people. Once you get past a certain point it might be hard to come back."*

In terms of dating, she articulated that *"when you are younger, guys think they're really cool, almost too cool for you. Then once they get older, they suddenly become less cool. Guys sometimes think they're the shit in high school, while girls are sort of going through an awkward phase. The benefit of getting older and learning from these experiences is you become more accepting of who you are and what you like."*

Now that she's matured into an independent young woman, Mary surrounds herself with people who are family-oriented, sweet, caring, complimentary, genuine, and fun to be around. She has learned that *"passion is very important, but sometimes passion can get confused with being blinded into an abusive or self-controlling. It is instead better to be lovable, sweet, and be nice."*

One of the most important statements Mary said about dating revolved around a person's behavior during arguments in relationships. She said it is important to "*have personal boundaries but* **don't say things when you are mad that you can't take back, because once you do, it's out there and can't be unsaid.**"

When discussing her own self-happiness, spending time with friends and family, creating art, going out to parties, concerts, the beach, and being adventurous are all aspects of life that make her feel like her happiest self. Being stagnant and not making memories is a fear of hers, which is why she wants to engage in more fun, happy, positive activities which would lead to creating more fulfilling memories.

CHAPTER 15

LIVING YOUR BEST LIFE

———

Life is short and uncertain. Nothing is guaranteed, but that's okay. We each face different, unique pressures that add stress to everyday lives. Life is not about comparing each other's problems in a "who has it the worst" competition. This is a time where we need to take a step back and be grateful for everything we have in our lives. Regardless of where we are, we each share at least one thing in common which is that we love somebody besides ourselves.

Whether it's a parent, sibling, or a friend, we learned to love someone else before it became time to love yourself. The reason why we need to love ourselves in the first place is so we can better take care of those who mean the most to us. By taking care of our own well-being, we can be more effective caregivers, friends, and lovers.

The people who love us unconditionally want to see us happy. By taking care of ourselves and fulfilling our own dreams, we are helping fulfill the dreams of those who love us most.

If you have read this book and still feel nervous, anxious, or not ready for the dating world, just remember to start off small and everything will work out.

Don't worry about rejection or take it personally. There have been many times in my life where romantic situations didn't work out, yet it was definitely for the better and I have started to realize that down the road.

Having friends of the opposite sex is extremely underutilized and comes with an unfortunate stigma. It is, however, a great way to understand yourself and what you will be looking for in a potential partner. They will give you the do's and don'ts as well as insider info that many boyfriends or girlfriends out there won't hear. Don't be the other guy and take advantage of their kindness—instead, use friendship to become a better person all around. In this life, you will begin to realize the opposite sex is not only there for you to date, but can become your best friends, the people you trust the most, but more importantly they can become part of your family.

A lot of dating comes from knowing yourself first. Derived from my own experience as well as the experiences of people I've interviewed, taking care of yourself first has resulted in much healthier relationships long term because the individuals involved are already happy with themselves. Taking time for self-discovery has led to more successful and long-lasting relationships, simply because they have found a partner who suits their needs versus their wants. By understanding yourself, you will begin to understand others in a more meaningful way.

Out of all the concepts we have talked about in this book thus far, I hope you become inspired to not only take care of yourself, but to also be more **empathetic** towards others (especially those closest to you). You never know what someone is truly going through unless you take the time to ask them. If you are under twenty-one and reading this, I hope you understand there are a lot of misconceptions in the world today and it will be your job to continue to ask questions. There are no absolutes, and not everything in the world is perfect. When you enter the dating scene as an adult, there is a lot more responsibility at stake. You will also begin to realize time is an incredible asset that should be used wisely.

CEO of Amazon Jeff Bezos developed a list of twelve important questions to ask yourself. Here's your chance to answer them.[33]

1. **How will you use your gifts?**

_____

_____

_____

2. **What choices will you make?**

_____

_____

_____

---

33 Tom Popomaronis, "Billionaire Jeff Bezos: To live a happy life with no regrets by age 80, ask yourself these 12 questions," *CNBC*, April 7, 2019.

3. Will inertia be your guide, or will you follow your passions?

   Passion → just do it, full frckin send it

4. Will you follow dogma, or will you be original?

   Be original → I want to be a badass PA and Professor

5. Will you choose a life of ease, or a life of service and adventure?

   I think all 3 can be combined

6. Will you wilt under criticism, or will you follow your convictions?

   Work through the criticism

7. Will you bluff it out when you're wrong, or will you apologize?

   Take responsibility

8. **Will you guard your heart against rejection, or will you act when you fall in love?**

   <u>I love love</u>

9. **Will you play it safe, or will you be a little bit swashbuckling?**

   <u>IDK what that word even mean but I know</u>
   <u>I prefer a calculated risk</u>

10. **When it's tough, will you give up or will you be relentless?**

    <u>Relentless adjuncted with therapy</u>

11. **Will you be a cynic, or will you be a builder?**

    <u>Just keep building like the distance</u>
    <u>runner I am</u>

12. **Will you be clever at the expense of others, or will you be kind?**

    <u>Follow my gut</u>

Don't think about the destination—enjoy the journey. Trust me, there were so many times where I was so focused on the end goal that once I achieved it, I realized I was not satisfied.

You will only become truly begin to experience self-love once you allow yourself to enjoy the process of internal growth.

> **You have complete control over every decision you make.** Don't let other people determine your happiness. Social media is not a reflection of your potential; it means nothing. When you die, your eulogy won't talk about how many followers you had or what your resume looked like. Instead, you will be remembered for the kind of person you were. **Always be yourself and learn to love and appreciate who you are.** There are people in this world who love you and want you to succeed. Do it for them! Love yourself because that's what the people who love you want.

This is your life! Live it the way you want and give along the way.

Thank You and God Bless

SOUL MATE QUIZ

Who Is Your Ideal Partner? The following questions are designed to help you journal your internal motivations, values, and desires when thinking about a potential long-term partner.

1) Name a place where you felt the happiest.

   In the woods or under my coat (Nature)

2) What do you love to do when you are alone?

   Listen to music, write

3) What are the top five qualities you value in a person?

   Honesty, loyalty

4) Why are you looking for a relationship?

   continous laughter and adventure, but a warm Sunday morning too

5) Do race, religion, or political affiliation matter to you? If so, explain why.

6) Are you willing to do an activity outside of your comfort zone to support your partner?

Yes

7) What was the longest relationship you have ever had? What did you learn about yourself?

I was abused and now I'm ready to end the cycle.

30-DAY VISION
FOR SELF-LOVE

———

The following vision is a series of recommended steps to help you find your best self through the art of **self-discovery**. Each activity takes only a few minutes at most; this is by no means a to-do list, but rather a guide which will help you set aside time for yourself. By the end of the 30-Day Vision, I hope you will learn something new about yourself and possibly develop some new habits along the way. **Enjoy the journey!**

Day 1: Forget about your responsibilities for just a few minutes. Make it a point that today you will do something just for you. This can be as general as possible.

Day 2: Think about a new habit or skill you would like to have in your life. Don't worry about implementing it yet; just think of ideas. They do not have to be specific or fit a certain criteria.

—ASL
- Swimming in the ocean

Day 3: Make today a day to do something new or out of your routine. It does not have to be something drastic as, say, "wake up at 4 a.m." Instead, try something you have not tried before.

Day 4: Reach out to a person you have not talked to in a while and see how they are doing.

Day 5: Cook a meal for yourself. It can be any kind of meal. Even if you cook every day for your family, take the time today to cook something for yourself. Enjoy it!

Day 6: Try a new form of exercise. Even it is for five minutes. Whether it's yoga, shadow boxing, or dance, just try it. More people should take the time to dance. By discovering how your body works, you'll open your mind further.

Day 7: Seek out a potential mentor. It may not happen right away but begin to think about people you look up to and would like to learn from. This can be done through a formal email or a much more casual message on social media. You'll be surprised at how many highly respected professionals will respond to you via social media messaging.

Day 8: Think about your inner circle and who you want in your life. If you plan on becoming successful or entering into the public eye, trust a select few to help you maintain your foundation. Your inner circle will also keep you humble and won't allow you to forget where you came from.

Day 9: Listen to a new album or playlist you haven't heard before. It sometimes can be easy to stick with listening to the same songs we love over and over again. Try something new! Perhaps a new genre, a genre undiscovered, could be your next go-to.

Day 10: Read a new book. Whether you are in the process of reading other books or haven't been reading at all, on this day pick up an entirely new book. Try to read for at least five minutes. You don't need to finish the whole book, just give it five minutes and you will learn something new in that short period of time.

Day 11: Be close to nature. Go out on a small expedition or to a place near your home. Take time to be close to nature even if it's for a few seconds. This will help get you out of your comfort zone and breathing in what the world has to offer.

Day 12: Clear your mind from negativity. Turn off your electronics for twenty minutes and calmly remove your doubts, fears, anxieties, and self-pressure. The health of your mind will be reflected in your actions. Try to practice positive thinking.

Day 13: Forgive someone. This is the time to let go! You don't need to officially send them a message, just do it internally. Removing the pain someone else caused you will allow you to move on and not dwell on people's past actions. The world is not perfect and will not treat you as such. In forgiveness, you will grow and blossom into the person you want to become.

Day 14: Draw a picture of an object, environment, or even a portrait. Engaging in the art of drawing will spark creativity and will allow you to feel calm and less stressed.

Day 15: Go out and give someone a generous tip. If it's at a local coffee shop, diner, or even a fast food restaurant, give someone a generous tip. You can help make someone's day. As a former waiter and busboy, getting an extra $3 to $5 really did put a smile on my face that day.

Day 16: Buy a meal for a homeless person. Try to make it a full meal, at least (sandwich, chips, and drink). It doesn't cost much (usually under $10) to brighten someone's day. Doing this will impact you and the person you are helping. You could be saving their life with just a simple gesture. Take a leap of faith and try it out! Also, spend time trying to get to know them (name, background, hobbies). Remember they are people too, and they deserve the same amount of socialization as we get.

Day 17: Take a moment to reflect. The previous two activities involved giving to others and not thinking about oneself. This is because if you truly want to experience happiness, you must help others. For today, just take a moment to reflect on your experiences over the past two days and think about what you have learned about yourself and other people.

Day 18: Begin thinking about investing for your future. This could be your 401K or figuring out your budget; everyone deserves financial independence, however only a few will make use of the resources available. Google has plenty of information to help you get started. Investing your money will make you money without you working.

Day 19: Reach out to a family member and tell them how much you love them. It can be any member of your family.

Make it sincere and take time to learn something new that's happening in their lives.

Day 20: Treat yourself. Whether it involves a glass (or a couple) of wine or going to your favorite coffee shop, give yourself a moment today where you can feel like your happiest self.

Day 21: Play a musical instrument. If you don't play an instrument, look up instruments you might be interested in learning. If you do play an instrument, make today your music day.

Day 22: Donate to a cause you are passionate about. Make it between five and ten dollars. There are many charitable fundraisers available on Facebook which are linked to credible organizations.

Day 23: Watch a speech on YouTube or any outlet that allows you do to so. Speeches can truly motivate self-improvement and embrace a call-to-action, especially with social movements. Take time to watch at least one speech of your choice. I highly recommend speeches of former presidents and civil rights leaders.

Day 24: Re-frame what you think about yourself. What is your opinion about yourself? Do you have a negative or positive self-image? What kind of person would you like to be? This is your chance to rewrite your script. Remember, you are the star in this movie called *Life*. What has been working versus what hasn't been working; take your time and make adjustments if needed. This can be done by choosing a new look or cultivating a new passion that gets you excited in the morning.

Day 25: Conquer your fear. Do something that scares you. No matter how little or big of a challenge it may be, accomplishing something that scares you can help free you from anxiety and build self-confidence. (Take your safety into consideration.)

~ Gina

Day 26: Develop your sense of style or fashion. Now, I strongly urge you take time to research and see what you genuinely like versus copying someone else's image. What makes a person unique is their taste. Be creative and become what you want to become.

Day 27: Emulate a role model. Who is someone you admire? What characteristics do they have that you could implement in your own life? You cannot copy their identity, but you can incorporate some of their positive traits into your life; there is nothing wrong with bettering yourself by looking at others as an example.

Day 28: Go on a long walk and think (music is optional). This is a great way not only to meditate but to also have some exercise in a relaxed state. If you can, find a park and chill there for a bit.

Day 29: Write a short positive message and place it in a location where you will see it every day. I recommend putting a message perhaps on your bathroom mirror or a place where you might see it when you wake up in the morning.

Day 30: Write yourself a letter. If you followed these steps, write what you learned about yourself when accomplishing these activities. There is no letter grade here. **Life is about finding what makes you happy.** No one else can do that for you besides you.

> *These activities don't need to be done in order—do as you please. This is designed to simply help you build momentum.

Enjoy the journey and never give up!

ACKNOWLEDGEMENTS

I would like to thank my **Lord and Savior Jesus Christ**,

My amazing Parents—The amount of love you have always showered on me has truly impacted me in ways words cannot describe. I owe you the world. I love you so much! You made me into the man I am today.

My Grandma—Thank you for always loving and supporting me.

Professor Abigail Marsh—Thank you so much for letting me interview you for this book. I had a fun time in our class and I learned a lot about myself, especially as a writer. Best wishes to your family. I watched your TED Talk as inspiration right before I recorded mine!

Alexis Krisak—You are a phenomenal person and your child is in great hands! Your husband is awesome, too. I hope to re-connect again! Much love.

Andrew Imbrie—Thank you for always giving advice, especially for my first book. Congratulations on your book! I can't wait to read it.

Ashton Nadine—Thank you for taking the time to give me an interview. I wish you positive vibes and best wishes in your future!

Casey Jones—Thank you for being supportive since the first day. You're truly one of the few people that I trust most and I can't thank you enough for your love and encouragement.

David & Devon—Thank you both for your endless generosity and love. It's sad I can't physically be there the way I want to, especially this past year. We are all trying to be productive and be put in a position to succeed, but there are moments when I just want to say "I love ya, bro" and give you a hug.

Daniel Kyle—Thanks for talking with me, man. I miss you and hope you come visit soon. Stay safe, brother!

Professor Donatella Lorch—Thank you for encouraging my writing. The moment I felt like a writer was not when my first book was published, but when you approved my final paper.

Emma Earnest—I'm glad we ran into each other that day in Georgetown. You've been there since my first book, first podcast episode, first TEDx Talk, and now this. I'm honored to have a strong woman like you in my life. Your messages of encouragement really helped me get through the hard parts of this journey. I believe in you! Thank you for your love and support. I am looking forward to our podcast together.

Eric Koester—This is all possible because of you. You continue to change the lives of this generation.

Faye Al-Saadoon—Thank you so much for supporting my book and podcast. You have a good heart. I believe in you! Stay positive and never give up.

Frankie Lange—Go Orioles! I love you brother. Keep the beard.

Hailey Lamb—I hope to see you at Nick's once life is back to normal. It's always fun to party with you!

Heather Wald—We go way back. Happy to see you still have the same heart. Love you, always.

Lauren Pallesen-Miller—Much love and thank you for supporting me. I wish you nothing but the best in everything you do!

Lexi Von Friedeburg—You are an angel! Thank for being there and supporting me when I gave my TEDx Talk. I wish you many blessing in your future!

Iliana Vazuka—You are a terrific person with all the talent in the world. I can't wait to watch you blossom at University of Chicago. I know you're going to make the most of this opportunity. I know that your father is extremely proud of you. He sounds like a terrific human being. Cheers to your success!

Jake Gilluly—I love you brother! I believe in you. Cheers!

Jenna Ryu—Thank you so much for reaching out and helping with this book. You have a bright future! Please take care of Douglas. Your *USA Today* article was awesome.

Johnny Lange—We have a ton of great memories. We are both trying to live the best lives possible. I am looking forward to finally re-connecting. I am proud of the work you're doing and best wishes to your tattoo shop. You are incredibly talented. I love you, brother. Happy Birthday.

Julian Graham—Yours was my favorite class at Georgetown, but my favorite part of that class was getting to know you.

Marshall Burke—I miss you, my man. We've had a ton of wild times and I miss all of them. I like your new hair and beard.

Mary Earley—You come from a lovely family, one that welcomed me with open arms. I'll be there when you make it big! Stay positive, because you can accomplish anything you set your mind to.

Michael James—I knew there was something special about you when we first met. I know that one day you will take the world by storm. I believe in you, brother. Bless!

Patricia Lindholm---You are an amazing friend and have always supported me and can't thank you enough. Much love!

Ricky & Matthew—My guys, we have been through quite a journey together. We all know the struggles and obstacles we had to face to get here.

Sigma Chi (Georgetown)—Best wishes to your careers. Stay positive and work hard! ΣΧ

Teddy Raymond—It was a ton of fun living with you. You are my brother now.

I wanted to do something a little different this time. I am giving thanks to those who helped along this journey. A lot has transpired since my first book. I learned a lot about myself and I am extremely grateful and fortunate to have such wonderful people in my life.

APPENDIX

INTRODUCTION

Battle, Nora. "Young People Are Staying Single For These 3 Reasons, According to New Research." *Thrive Global*, October 10, 2018. *https://thriveglobal.com/stories/young-people-are-staying-single-for-these-3-reasons-according-to-new-research.*

Bote, Joshua. "Millennial and Gen Z singles have enough casual sex. But they want love, survey says." *USA Today*, July 29, 2019. *https://www.usatoday.com/story/news/nation/2019/07/29/match-singles-survey-millennials-gen-z-want-love-have-sex/1861101001.*

CHAPTER 1

Burzumato, Skip. "A Brief History of Courtship and Dating in America, Part 2." *Boundless*, March 8, 2007. *https://www.boundless.org/relationships/a-brief-history-of-courtship-and-dating-in-america-part-2/.*

Fetters, Ashley. "The Five Years That Changed Dating." *The Atlantic*, December 21, 2018. *https://www.theatlantic.com/family/archive/2018/12/tinder-changed-dating/578698/.*

Fry, Richard. Kristen Bialik. "Millennial life: How young adulthood today compares with prior generations." Pew Research Center, Accessed February 14, 2019. *https://www.pewsocialtrends.org/essay/millennial-life-how-young-adulthood-today-compares-with-prior-generations/.*

CHAPTER 2

Garfield, Leanna. "What it's like to use Siren, the new dating app that aims to be classier than Tinder." *Business Insider,* October 17, 2016. *https://www.businessinsider.com/siren-review-new-dating-app-tinder-2016-10/.*

Marateck, Juliet. "Online dating lowers self-esteem and increases depression, studies say." *CNN,* May 29, 2018. *https://www.cnn.com/2018/05/29/health/online-dating-depression-study/index.html/.*

Soper, Taylor. "Dating app Siren, which empowered women, shuts down after running out of money." *GeekWire*, April 5, 2017. *https://www.geekwire.com/2017/dating-app-siren-empowered-women-shuts-running-money/.*

CHAPTER 3

Bloomberg Quick Take Originals. "Japan, Virtual Partners Fill Romantic Void." September 22, 2017. Video, 1:03. *https://www.youtube.com/watch?v=1FIOcIDM5Uo.*

Imperial College Business School. "The Future of Dating 2040." *eHarmony*, Published November 2015. *https://www.eharmony.co.uk/dating-advice/wp-content/uploads/2015/11/eHarmony.co_.uk-Imperial-College-Future-of-Dating-Report-20401.pdf.*

Marketwatch. "How AI and video could transform the online dating industry." May 3, 2018. Video, 1:24. *https://www.*

marketwatch.com/video/sectorwatch/how-ai-and-video-
could-transform-the-online-dating-industry/FB396236-D2CF-
44F5-B7B5-CD6A27580AEA.html.

Myers, Quinn. "Futurists Predict What Online Dating Will Look Like in 10 years." *Melmagazine*, December 11, 2018. *https://melmagazine.com/en-us/story/futurists-predict-what-online-dating-will-look-like-in-10-years/.*

Vadnal, Julie. "The Future of Dating: Where Relationships Are Heading." *Bumble*, 2020. *https://bumble.com/the-buzz/future-of-dating-where-relationships-are-heading.*

CHAPTER 4

EWTN. "World Over-2018-04-12-'The Dating Project,' Dr. Kerry Cronin with Raymond Arroyo." April 13, 2018. Video, 9:12. *https://www.youtube.com/watch?v=lPiDFomrALk.*

Goleman, Daniel. Richard Boyateis, and Anne Mckee. "On Emotional Intelligence: Primal Leadership." Boston: Harvard Business Review Press, 2015.

Rosenfeld, Michael. "Who wants the Breakup? Gender and Breakup in Heterosexual Couples." *Stanford*. Published 2017. *https://web.stanford.edu/~mrosenfe/Rosenfeld_gender_of_breakup.pdf.*

CHAPTER 5

Achor, Shawn. The Happiness Advantage. New York: Crown, 2010.

TED. "The new era of positive psychology | Martin Seligman." July 21, 2008. Video, 9:34. *https://www.youtube.com/watch?v=9F-Bxfd7DL3E.*

CHAPTER 6

Botelho, L. Elena. Kim R. Powell. The CEO Next Door. New York: Currency Publishing, 2018.

Wade, Francis. "Can Happiness Be Created With Proper Time Management?" *Lifehack*, Accessed 2020. *https://www.lifehack.org/articles/productivity/can-happiness-be-synthesized-with-proper-time-management.html.*

CHAPTER 7

Dalio, Ray. "Principles." New York: Simon & Schuster, 2017.

Marsh, Abigail. "Fear Factor." New York: Basic Books, 2017.

CHAPTER 8

Dwyer, Chris. "The world's most romantic places." *CNN*, February 14, 2020. *https://www.cnn.com/travel/article/romantic-places/index.html.*

Vishnevskaya, Irina. "Your Honeymoon Is More Important Than Your Wedding—Here's Why." *HuffPost*, October 23, 2017. *https://www.huffpost.com/entry/your-honeymoon-is-more-important-than-your-wedding_b_59ed3acce4b034105edd4fee.*

CHAPTER 9

Duckworth, Angela. "Grit." New York: Scribner, 2016.

Duhigg, Charles. "The Power of Habit." New York: Random House, 2014.

Shallenberger, R. Steven. "Becoming Your Best." McGraw Hill Education, 2015.

CHAPTER 10

N/A

CHAPTER 11

Carra, Tita. "Will Smith Explains Why It's Not His Responsibility To Make His Wife Happy."

Goggins, David. "Can't Hurt Me." Lioncrest Publishing. 2018.

Haute Living, February 21, 2018. *https://hauteliving.com/2018/02/ will-smith-jada-pinkett-smith/651889.*

CHAPTER 12

N/A

CHAPTER 13

Brenner, Abigail. "10 Relationship Red Flags." *Psychologytoday.* July 29, 2014. *https://www.psychologytoday.com/us/blog/in-flux /201407/10-relationship-red-flags?page=1.*

Schuller, Robert. "Hours of Power," New York: HarperSanfrancisco. 2014.

Sternberg, J. Robert. "Duplex Theory of Love: Triangular Theory of Love and Theory of Love as a Story." *Robertjsternberg*, Accessed 2020. *http://www.robertjsternberg.com/love.*

CHAPTER 14

N/A

CHAPTER 15

Popomaronis, Tom. "Billionaire Jeff Bezos: To live a happy life with no regrets by age 80, ask yourself these 12 questions." *CNBC*, April 7, 2019. *https://www.cnbc.com/2019/04/05/amazon-billionaire-ceo-jeff-bezos-ask-yourself-these-12-questions-to-live-a-long-happy-life.html*.

SOUL MATE QUIZ

N/A

30-DAY VISION FOR SELF-LOVE

N/A

Made in the USA
Columbia, SC
25 February 2021